To: My boss

Subject: This book, "Busting Bureaucracy"

❑   I read this book, and I think it describes our
     organization—at least a little. I'd like to get your
     thoughts.

❑   I read this book, and I think it has a lot to offer our
     organization. If you agree, feel free to pass it on to
     others.

❑   This book supports our (Quality) (Service) campaign,
     and reinforces how important it is. What do you think
     about getting the whole management team a copy?
     We could even get one for everyone in the organization,
     if you agree. (There's a section just for managers and
     one just for front-line people.)

❑   I was so excited about this book that I ordered a bunch
     to pass around. Please read it and lets talk.

❑   _____

     _____

Signed _____

BUSTING BUREAUCRACY

How to Conquer Your Organization's Worst Enemy

BUSTING BUREAUCRACY

How to Conquer Your Organization's Worst Enemy

Kenneth B. Johnston

BUSINESS ONE IRWIN
Homewood, Illinois 60430

Senior editor: Jeffrey A. Krames
Project editor: Karen J. Nelson
Production manager: Mary Jo Parke
Designer: Heidi J. Baughman
Printer: R. R. Donnelley & Sons Company

Library of Congress Cataloging-in-Publication Data

Johnston, Kenneth B.
    Busting bureaucracy : how to conquer your organization's worst enemy / Kenneth B. Johnston.
        p.   cm.
    ISBN 1-55623-878-9
    1. Organizational effectiveness   2. Bureaucracy.   I. Title.
HD58.9.J64   1993
658—dc20   92-6713

Printed in the United States of America

1 2 3 4 5 6 7 8 9 0 DOC 9 8 7 6 5 4 3 2

This book is dedicated to you who work in a bureaucratic organization and would prefer to work in a more healthful, productive and satisfying work environment.

Acknowledgments

I wish to acknowledge the many people who have inspired, encouraged, helped and guided me through the creation of this book.

My wife, friend and partner, Shannon Johnston, helped the most.

I've been inspired by Tom Peters, Ron Zemke, Karl Albrecht, Jan Carlzon, Frederick Herzberg, Abraham Maslow, Thomas Harris and many other visionaries whose ideas have become so ingrained in my thinking that I wove their work in with mine without giving them adequate credit.

I've borrowed liberally from the experiences of my fellow consultants, Juan Gutierrez, Ron Cox, Vicki Silvers, John Iacovini, Nancy Hensel, Tom Canty, Virginia Townsley, Jerry Plec and many others.

Bill Salzer, Lois Meredith, Thomas Hamm, Debra Grundy, Kathy Cook-Farzanegan, Erin LaMonte, Kim Zee, Peg Anthony, Chuck Lalonde, Gary Richardson and many others got me together with their customers so I could learn directly from real-life people working in real-life bureaucracies.

Whole chapters have been inspired by the thought-provoking questions of Deborah Chapman.

Jeffrey Krames, Barbara Glanz, Sarah Kruse and Jennifer Guidry all helped make the book more readable.

Andrea Jensen took my messed-up manuscript and made it into a book.

Don Baumgart's cartoons bring the foibles of bureaucracy to life and make me laugh every time I see one.

Dick Woltmann suffered through many evenings listening to these ideas and helping me work them out.

Dave Erdman did all of my work so I could spend time working on this book.

And finally, I would like to recognize the many wonderful people who helped me understand what it is really like to live in a bureaucratic organization.

Understandably, those who have helped me the most don't want me to mention them or their organizations by name. Somehow, it isn't yet politically correct to be recognized as being an expert on bureaucracy. Nor do many organizations wish to be identified as examples of bureaucracy in action. I hope you will recognize your contributions as you read the book. You know who you are, and I am ever in your debt.

Foreword

My study of bureaucracy has been more accidental than planned.

For more than thirty years, I have been privileged to be on the "inside" of hundreds of large organizations. For ten years, I was with IBM helping large organizations absorb their first computers. For the past nineteen years, I have been part of Kaset International, whose mission is to help organizations achieve extraordinary customer relations.

My work has always involved helping organizations change. Whether they were absorbing their first computer, or working to become "customer focused," I came to know them when they were dealing with significant change.

Virtually every organization I worked with had some of the negative "stuff" that most of us informally call "bureaucracy." Some were very bureaucratic. Some were less so. Frankly, the stuff we call bureaucracy was so omnipresent that I just took it for granted.

Then, something odd began to happen. I noticed that whenever an organization decided to undertake a service quality improvement program, they also reported a reduction in the stuff they called bureaucracy.

In the early stages, I even thought that service improvement campaigns were, by themselves, a method of reducing bureaucracy.

Unfortunately, it turned out that the de-bureaucratizing effects of service improvement were not permanent. In fact, I observed that *service improvement* efforts were being thwarted by bureaucracy. More recently, I have also observed that many, if not most, *quality* improvement efforts are also being thwarted by bureaucracy.

From these observations, I offer the following assertions:

- In the early stages of an effort to become "customer focused," the negative effects of bureaucracy are noticeably reduced.

- In the later stages of an effort to become customer focused, bureaucracy becomes the primary barrier.

By 1985, I had realized that many, if not most, of the organizations I worked with needed help to reduce or eliminate bureaucracy. After researching everything I could find on bureaucracy, I discovered that many writers had written about what bureaucracy is, but very little had been written about how to reduce or eliminate it.

Thus was born this book.

Table of Contents

Introduction

Preview

This introduction presents, in summary form, some conclusions and assertions that are developed throughout the book. In addition, you will find some exciting possibilities, along with some provocative, and even outrageous, statements. One purpose is to stimulate you to want to read the book. The other is to offer easily found book-bites to critics and talk show hosts.

A summary of conclusions

• The bureaucratic organizing model is the most common organizing model for private and public sector organizations throughout the world. The bureaucratic model does not produce organizations that are extraordinary at satisfying customers or achieving "quality" in their products.

• A number of Japanese companies have, almost inadvertently, modified the basic bureaucratic model, and have been able to competitively dominate many of the world's unmodified bureaucratic business organizations.

• Businesses throughout the industrialized world, reacting to increasingly global competition, are seeking to become "customer focused," or are adopting some form of "Total Quality Management." In the early stages, both TQM and becoming "customer focused" reduce the negative symptoms of bureaucracy. Eventually, however, the underlying bureaucracy becomes the biggest barrier to these organizations achieving their goal. At some point, these organizations will be forced to confront the fact that they are organized based on the bureaucratic model.

• Monopoly is the major ally of bureaucracy. Bureaucracies can only succeed when protected by tariffs, patents, copyrights, market positioning, oligopoly, or outright monopoly. In truly competitive arenas, unmodified bureaucratic organizations seldom earn the customer satisfaction needed to compete.

• Bureaucracy seems to be the organizational form that produces the highest levels of personal satisfaction for those at the top of an organization. It seems that virtually every organization that is protected from market forces eventually becomes more and more bureaucratic.

On the other hand, in a free market, less bureaucratic organizations put competitive pressure on bureaucratic organizations until they are forced to become market driven to survive.

In other words, organizations tend to become bureaucratic when they are allowed to, but will be market driven when forced to by competition.

• Government agencies represent the worst of all possible combinations. Each agency is given some form of monopoly. Each agency is organized as a bureaucracy. It should be no surprise that government agencies come in dead last when consumers are asked to evaluate organizations in terms of "productivity," "quality" or "service."

The tragic results are evident everywhere. The people in government are blamed for the poor results, yet they are victims of a poor organizing model. The citizens get poor results for their taxes, and they blame it on politicians or people in government. Politicians do their best to bring about meaningful change, and their efforts are defeated by government workers trapped in a system immobilized by bureaucracy. It is time to recognize the real villain, the bureaucratic organizing model. Citizens, politicians, appointees and government workers are all victimized by bureaucracy.

Assertions and observations

• The successful Japanese companies are powerful but vulnerable. Even though they have modified bureaucracy, most Japanese companies are still organized using the basic bureaucratic form. I assert that those large, bureaucratic organizations can be overtaken by "mission driven" organizations that are flexible, responsive, innovative, and have "customer friendly" policies, practices and procedures.

• With the possible exception of a few governmental agencies, I believe that the bureaucratic form is NEVER the best organizing form. In case I'm not being clear enough, let me say this.

I believe there is no legitimate reason for any public or private sector organization that aspires to quality products or customer-satisfying service to continue using the bureaucratic organizational form.

• Many Western organizations, in both the private and public sectors, are installing "quality" programs as part of their search for excellence (as well as a cure for the symptoms of bureaucracy). Most are using some form of "shadow" organization (steering committees, task forces, action teams, etc.) to implement "quality" in their organizations. I predict that the organizations' underlying bureaucracy will defeat these efforts unless the shadow organizations are organized in a "mission-driven" form (a non-bureaucratic form described in this book). To be clear, having observed many cases, we have never seen a bureaucratically organized shadow organization cure a bureaucratic organization of poor quality or service.

• The employees of bureaucratic organizations suffer the most. The more bureaucratic the organization is, the more stress, anxiety, and anger the employees have.

• Organizational health and success in the future may depend more on organizational structure than on access to capital and market monopolies.

Exciting possibilities

• We have alternatives to entrusting our most difficult national issues to bureaucratic governmental agencies. We can make it possible for some of our government agencies to become mission driven, (a non-bureaucratic organizing form described herein). And, we can allow more competition from the private sector to stimulate governmental de-bureaucratization in critical areas.

• The Eastern bloc nations that are building private enterprises from scratch, and Third World nations seeking a place in the global economy have the opportunity to bypass bureaucracy as their organizing model. They can begin as "mission-driven" organizations. If they do that, the successful ones will be able to catch and pass the rest of the world's unmodified bureaucratic organizations.

• Mission-driven organizations represent the future and the hope of Third World nations. Bypassing bureaucracy as their organizing model will allow Third World organizations to start small, with limited capital, and accumulate capital as they grow profitably through market acceptance, rather than relying on the extensive capital and market monopolies required for success with the bureaucracy model.

• I believe that a combination of private enterprise and purposeful de-bureaucratization will make it possible to overcome the bureaucratic paralysis that immobilizes public education in the United States. My book, "De-bureaucratize Please!" written for people in government, offers a vision of a "customer-focused" education system. This vision is so powerful and so compelling that I predict the bureaucratic educational system will adopt it and bring it to life, or else the citizenry will "privatize" education, and replace the existing educational system and its bureaucracy.

Provocative and/or outrageous statements

• Max Weber has done as much economic and social damage by idealizing bureaucracy as Marx and Lenin did by attacking capitalism and promoting communism.

• Bureaucracy and communism are two models for organizing enterprises that sound good on paper, but produce really rotten results.
• The single greatest cause for the failure of communism was that communism was organized based on the bureaucratic model, thus creating suffocating and immobilizing bureaucracies.

• Bureaucracy has killed communism. It has socialism in a death grip, and is suffocating and immobilizing every capitalistic organization that adopts its false promises.
• Unions will change or die. Unions depend on alienation between workers and the organizations in which they work. To produce quality products or deliver extraordinary customer satisfaction, workers must become team members in unified, mission-driven organizations that cannot be divided against themselves. Given the reality of global competition, the only organizations that will be able to survive with alienated work forces will be those with some form of monopoly.

- Unions may continue to have a role to play in healthy, non-monopolistic organizations, but to play that role they will have to become aligned with the mission and help to support the mission, rather than be a divisive influence. The future of the union lies in healing rather than creating worker alienation. If unions are to have any viable role, union leaders and their organizations need to be supported by stakeholders so that they create worker harmony that supports the organization's mission.

Summary

In this introduction, you've found some well-grounded conclusions as well as some outrageous assertions. I trust your judgment in deciding which is which. If the introduction has served to whet your appetite for the rest of the book, then it is has served it's purpose. If it hasn't, then you've saved several hours. If it's done neither, then please disregard it.

Chapter One

An executive summary: the book in a nutshell

Preview

This chapter serves as a summary of the entire book. The purpose is to give you an overview of what is contained in the book. It describes the goals of the book and serves as a preview of what the book covers.

This book is intended for people who work in bureaucratic organizations. It is designed to be circulated among managers to stimulate dialog, build commitment and facilitate decisions regarding possible changes to the organization. It is also designed to be given to people who are currently not managing so they might participate in the decision to change, or so they will understand any change effort that the management team decides to undertake.

The goal of the book is to help you learn the following:

1. Your organization is almost certainly organized using much or all of what is called the "bureaucratic form."

2. Virtually all organizations that use the bureaucratic form seem to suffer the same suffocating and immobilizing symptoms that people call "bureaucracy."

3. Most employees blame their organization's "bureaucracy" on senior management. They assume that management must want it, or it wouldn't be tolerated.

4. Senior managers don't want or like "bureaucracy" any more than the rest of the employees. The detestable effects of bureaucracy victimize everyone, regardless of level. Senior managers haven't known what to do to get rid of it. Executives have tried many things to eliminate "bureaucracy," but the "program-of-the-year" approach generally hasn't worked, because they have been fighting symptoms, not the root cause.

5. The root cause of "bureaucracy" is the organizing model, the "bureaucratic form." Yet, the bureaucratic form is so pervasive that its destructive nature is seldom questioned.

6. If you were starting a new enterprise today, you could avoid "bureaucracy" by using a new organizing model called the "mission-driven" model.

7. Existing bureaucratic organizations can reduce the amount of "bureaucracy" by changing one or more of the basic organizing principles, either temporarily or permanently. This book outlines a set of steps for de-bureaucratizing by changing basic organizing principles:

    a. Make an assessment of the present state of the organization to learn how much permission to change and commitment to

change is available from stakeholders and senior management.

b. Depending on the amount of available commitment, choose
the optimal goal state: a modest goal, a moderate goal, or an
ambitious goal.

c. The goal state will suggest the strategy for changing the organization. The strategy will range from a minimum effort
based mostly on training to a maximum effort based on reorganization and a new way of managing called "continuous
improvement."

d. Continuous improvement is an entirely new way of operating in which the people closest to the product or customer,
working in teams, are empowered to continuously improve
the organization's quality, service, or both. Continuous improvement requires three things:

1. A "shadow" organization chartered to make the changes
necessary in the existing organization to achieve the desired goal state.

2. New forms of qualitative customer feedback from internal
and external customers to be used to drive changes in
quality, service, or both.

3. Training for employees enabling them to work in teams,
to accept the offered empowerment, to identify and prioritize root causes of problems, and to find solutions they
will use to continuously improve quality, service, or both.

8. Management people in the existing organization will need to
learn and use new ways of managing. They will need to learn
what they have been doing that adds to the "bureaucracy" in the
organization. They will need to learn new ways of doing their
jobs that diminish the amount of bureaucracy within the organization. Most importantly, they will need to provide empowerment for those who work for them, and protection and
coaching to those who accept and act upon the offered empowerment.

9. People in the organization who currently aren't managing will
play a vital new role in the de-bureaucratized organization. The
labor/management war, if it exists in your organization, must

end. Everyone in the organization will need to act as one unified team, driven by a common mission, and aligned by a common vision of the new organization. People who today are not formally managing will be grouped into teams in which the brainpower, skills, talents, and experience of the individuals will be harnessed to continuously improve the organization's quality, service, or both.

People who are presently not in managerial positions will be drawn to enroll in the change effort because their new, expanded role offers less bureaucracy and more opportunity for motivation through personal growth, achievement, responsibility, recognition and more interesting work.

10. Finally, the book closes with a vision of what your organization might look like, and be like, when you have achieved your desired goal state. You will discover the rewards that come from working in an organization of empowered people who are satisfying or even dazzling their customers, and are doing so with few, if any, of the immobilizing and suffocating effects of bureaucracy.

Chapter Two

The word bureaucracy and its multiple meanings

Preview

This chapter explains the bureaucratic form, which is the basic organizing form for public sector organizations and for most private sector organizations as well. You will learn the basic principles of the form and the advantages offered by the form.

The word **bureaucracy** has at least three different meanings:

1. **A group of workers** (for example, civil service employees of the U. S. government) is referred to as "the bureaucracy." An example: "The threat of Gramm-Rudman-Hollings cuts has **the bureaucracy** in Washington deeply concerned."

2. Bureaucracy is the name of **an organizational form** used by sociologists and organizational design professionals.

3. Bureaucracy has an **informal** usage, as in "there's too much bureaucracy where I work." This informal usage describes a set of characteristics or attributes such as "red tape" or "inflexibility" that frustrate people who deal with or who work for organizations they perceive as "bureaucratic."

Throughout this book, I'll use the following conventions:

1. When I'm talking about **a group of people,** I'll always use "the bureaucracy," or "bureaucrats."

2. When I'm talking about the organizational form, I'll always link the word *form* with the word bureaucratic or bureaucracy. (No matter how clumsy that becomes.)

3. Therefore, when you see the word bureaucracy or bureaucratic—by itself—then it describes the negative attributes—the "stupidity," the "nonsense" that you and I mean when we talk about having "too much bureaucracy."

The "bureaucratic form..."

As you read about the bureaucratic form, note whether your organization matches the description. The more of these concepts that exist in your organization, the more likely you will have some or all of the negative by-products described in the next chapter.

Max Weber, a German sociologist, wrote in the 1930s a rationale that described the bureaucratic form as being the ideal way of organizing government agencies.

The bureaucratic form and its use spread throughout both public and the private sectors. Even though Weber's writings have been widely discredited, the bureaucratic form lives on.

The bureaucratic form has six major principles.

1. *A formal hierarchical structure*
   Each level controls the level below and is controlled by the level above. A formal hierarchy is the basis of central planning and centralized decision making.

2. *Management by rules*
   Controlling by rules allows decisions made at high levels to be executed consistently by all lower levels.

3. *Organization by functional specialty*
   Work is to be done by specialists, and people are organized into units based on the type of work they do or skills they have.

4. *An "up-focused" or "in-focused" mission*
   If the mission is described as "up-focused," then the organization's purpose is to serve the stockholders, the board, or whatever agency empowered it. If the mission is to serve the organization itself, and those within it, e.g., to produce high profits, to gain market share, or to produce a cash stream, then the mission is described as "in-focused."

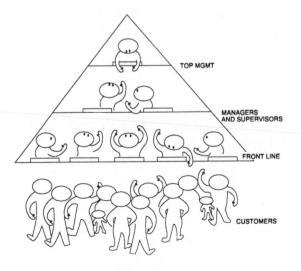

In-Focused Organization

5. *Purposely impersonal*
   The idea is to treat all employees equally and customers equally, and not be influenced by individual differences.

6. *Employment based on technical qualifications*
   (There may also be protection from arbitrary dismissal.)

The bureaucratic form according to Parkinson has another attribute.

7. *Predisposition to grow in staff "above the line."*
   Weber failed to notice this, but C. Northcote Parkinson found it so common that he made it the basis of his humorous "Parkinson's law." Parkinson demonstrated that the management and professional staff tends to grow at predictable rates, almost without regard to what the line organization is doing.

The bureaucratic form is so common that most people accept it as the normal way of organizing almost any endeavor. People in bureaucratic organizations generally blame the ugly side effects of bureaucracy on management, or the founders, or the owners, without awareness that the real cause is organizing based on the bureaucratic form. After all, the bureaucratic form has been so common because it promises some major benefits.

The major benefits promised by the bureaucratic form.

Hierarchical authority promises control and responsibility.

According to organizational design theory, the top executive would have control over the entire organization, and the outside world would know who to hold responsible. "The captain of the ship is responsible for whatever happens on or to the ship."

Remember, in the 1920s and 1930s when bureaucracy was beginning to flower, the world of business and government was very different than today. Today's industrialized nations were switching from agrarian societies to industrial societies. Prior to industrialization, organizations tended to be smaller, education and experience had not been so available or important, and management skills were seldom required, except at the very top.

So, in an organization in which the senior people were educated—and the workers were less so—it seemed vital to concentrate on control.

Management by rules promises control and consistency

If the entire organization was managed by rules, then top management could be sure that the organization would be controlled by their decisions. And, top management could be sure that no arbitrary "judgment" was introduced into the operation to make things inconsistent. The top executive could decide how things would be done, and forever after they would be done that way.

Consistency seemed desirable because the world prior to the industrial revolution was marked by inconsistency. People were discriminated against because of class, education, race, religion or creed. People were given advantages because of wealth, class or education. In a world where people were treated very differently from one another, consistency must have seemed very desirable.

An up-focused mission promised that governmental agencies would serve the legislative or executive bodies that formed them.

The idea seemed sound, because it promised that an agency of government wouldn't end up serving the people who were in the agency, nor would it end up serving people outside of the agency. Instead, theoretically, it would serve the government—hence, all the people.

In corporations, an up-focused mission promised that the organization would serve the stockholders, represented by the board of directors, rather than the people within the organization.

Specialization of sub-units promised accountability, control and expertise.

If specialists were in charge of each function of the organization, then top management could be certain that an educated or trained person was responsible for that function. In addition, top management could be reasonably certain that the people handling that function were *expert* in that function. Both of these benefits promised more certain control and effectiveness.

Prior to the twentieth century, people were given responsibility for managing most often because of their wealth, class or family— not necessarily because they were trained or skilled. So, having specialists handle functions seemed like a big improvement over having people manage things because they were the boss's son, or the family had contacts.

Being impersonal promises objectivity, consistency and equality.

The theory suggests that if you wipe out the human elements of the business transaction, and focus only on the "business" side, that you could be sure that no customer or citizen was treated better or worse than another. If you treat everyone identically, as though they had no individual differences, then you could ensure fairness through equal treatment. You could also ensure consistency.

This was highly valued in those days because many people felt they didn't get treated equally with those of wealth, power or position. In the various European and North American cultures of the early twentieth century, customers were not always treated equally by businesses, and citizens were not treated equally by government. Bureaucracy promised fairness and equality.

Employment based on technical qualifications promises equal opportunity, and protection from arbitrary dismissal promises job security to those who can pass a test and follow the rules.

Equal opportunity meant that a middle class educated person had the same opportunity of entry into government as an upper class or wealthy person. That was highly valued in an era when government tended to be controlled or dominated by those with money, power or position.

Job security was little known in the early twentieth century, but highly valued and highly prized. Bureaucracy promised protection against arbitrary dismissal. People with wealth, power or position exerted powerful control over businesses and government. Workers were subject to arbitrary dismissal if they offended the wrong people.

Summary

• The bureaucratic form evolved in a different era, and promised to solve different problems than those that exist today.

Chapter Three

"Bureaucracy"
...the negative by-products

Preview

In this chapter, you'll find the organizational symptoms that customers and employees describe as "bureaucracy." You'll see a comparison between what the bureaucratic form promises and what it delivers, and you'll learn how the destructive by-products we call "bureaucracy" are almost certainly caused by using the bureaucratic organizing form.

In nineteen years of interviewing customers and employees of public corporations, I've heard the words "bureaucracy" and "bureaucratic" used to describe a wide range of behaviors, attitudes and decisions:

- Customers call an organization "bureaucratic" when it has rigid policies and procedures that customers describe as "red tape."

- Customers describe an organization as "bureaucratic" when its policies don't satisfy the customer's individual situation, and the employees take refuge behind the idea that the policy is the same for all customers.

- Customers say an organizations is "bureaucratic" when the organization seems inflexible and unresponsive to a customer's individual situation.

- Customers describe organizations as "bureaucratic" when the organization has standard procedures, policies or practices that seem designed solely for the benefit of the organization and which work to the disadvantage of customers.

- Customers think of organizations as bureaucratic when the organization makes it seem very difficult to get exceptions approved.

- Customers link "bureaucratic" and "uncaring," e.g., they complain of being treated more like "numbers" than individuals.

- Customers think of an organization as "bureaucratic" when the organization is unwilling to admit mistakes and attempts to shift blame for their own mistakes onto the customer.

- Customers often link the word "bureaucratic" with the idea of not being innovative. When asked to explain what it means to be "bureaucratic," they'll often mention that bureaucratic organizations are slow to innovate, and seem reluctant to change as times change or events dictate.

- Once customers characterize an organization as bureaucratic, they also tend to believe that the organization has products and services of inferior quality (compared with non-bureaucratic organizations).

- Customers describe organizations that are hard to reach during company hours, and that during busy periods may hardly be reachable at all, as "bureaucratic." Once again, they associate lack of access with being bureaucratic, and they cite inaccessibility as an example of "not caring."

- Customers of companies described as "bureaucratic" frequently characterize those organizations as being "arrogant" and "lacking in a sense of humor."

- Customers associate the following things with organizations they characterize as "bureaucratic."

  a. Getting transferred around a number of times when they call.

  b. Employees who are not positive about the organization. They give the impression that they aren't happy to be working there.

  c. Employees who are less than enthusiastic about the organization's products or services.

  d. Employees who aren't friendly, and give the impression they don't care if the customer is satisfied or not.

Inside the organization, employees live with some very negative by-products of the bureaucratic form.

When employees are asked to give examples of things they think of as being bureaucratic, they frequently cite the following:

- Each department has its own agenda, and departments don't cooperate to help other departments get the job done.

- The head of a department feels responsible first for protecting the department, its people and its budget, even before helping to achieve the organization's mission.

- There is political in-fighting, with executives striving for personal advancement and power.

- Ideas can be killed because they come from the "wrong" person. Ideas will be supported because the are advanced by the "right" person.

- People in their own department spend much of their time protecting their department's "turf."

- People in *other* departments spend so much time protecting their "turf" that they don't have time to do the work they are responsible to do.

- They are treated as though they can't be trusted.

- They are treated as though they don't have good judgment.

- They are treated as though they won't work hard unless pushed.

- Their work environment includes large amounts of unhealthy stress.

- The tendency of the organization is to grow top-heavy, while the operating units of the organization tend to be too lean.

- Promotions are more likely to be made on the basis of politics, rather than actual achievements on the job.

- Top managers are dangerously ill-informed and insulated from what is happening on the front lines or in "the field."

- Information is hoarded or kept secret and used as the basis for power.

- Data is used selectively, or distorted to make performance look better than it really is.

- Internal communications to employees are distorted to reflect what the organization would like to be, rather than what it really is.

- Mistakes and failures are denied, covered up or ignored.

- Responsibility for mistakes and failure tends to be denied, and where possible, blame is shifted to others.

- Decisions are made by larger and larger groups, so no one can be held accountable.

- Decisions are made based on the perceived desires of superiors, rather than concern for mission achievement.

- Policies, practices and procedures tend to grow endlessly and to be followed more and more rigidly.

- Senior managers become so insulated from the realities of the front line that they may use stereotypical thinking and out-of-date experience in making decisions.

- Quantitative measurements are favored over qualitative measurements, so the concentration is on quantities of output, with less and less concern for quality of output.

- Both employees and customers are treated more as numbers than people. Personal issues and human needs are ignored or discounted.

Summary

• "Bureaucracy" as defined by customers and employees is an array of negative forces, attitudes or actions that are damaging to customer and employee satisfaction.

• "Bureaucracy" is damaging to organizational effectiveness. It weakens employee morale and commitment. It divides people within the organization against each other, and misdirects their energy into conflict or competition with each other instead of mission achievement.

• The negative organizational symptoms we call "bureaucracy" are almost certainly derived from organizing based on the bureaucratic form.

Chapter Four

Does the bureaucratic form live up to its promises?

Preview

This chapter compares the promises of the bureaucratic form with the realities that exist in bureaucracies. The bureaucratic form promises some wonderful advantages. This chapter examines those promises, and finds that the reality falls far short. Those readers who live and work in bureaucratic organizations will most likely find that this chapter affirms their everyday work experiences.

Promises *vs.* realities

The control that is promised by the bureaucratic model turns out to be illusory, and quite limited.

One of the first lessons that CEOs learn is that the "control" they had hoped for turns out to be an illusion. As CEO, you can usually stop something from happening. You can stop projects. You can stop things from growing. You can even stop some behaviors. The problem is, in the well-formed bureaucracy, it is more difficult for the CEO to "start" things, or make good things happen. As a result, the bureaucratic model allows the senior managers to "not do" certain kinds of things, but isn't as helpful in getting the organization to "do" things.

For example, CEOs who want to make their organizations "customer focused" or to employ "total quality management" find either virtually impossible to achieve unless they let go of the bureaucratic model and begin using principles from other organizing models. The evidence is abundantly clear that the bureaucratic model will not give the CEO or senior managers enough "control" to transform their organization into producing world class quality or dazzling customer satisfaction.

The responsibility and accountability that are promised by the bureaucratic model are easily and often subverted.

Anyone who has been in a bureaucracy for more than a couple of weeks quickly learns the different ways to avoid responsibility or accountability. The strategies range from not doing anything, to taking no risks, to stifling innovation, or to getting many additional signatures.

There are literally dozens of ways to avoid responsibility and accountability. So, the bureaucratic organizing model doesn't produce accountability. In fact, I suggest it does exactly the opposite. Fully formed bureaucracies penalize people for taking responsibility and being accountable.

The equal opportunity promised by the bureaucratic model is easily and often subverted.

There are some huge bureaucracies today, in private industry and in the public sector, which promise equal opportunity, but don't deliver. On the other hand, it should also be noted that governmental bureaucracies have led the way in making equal opportunity a reality. So, it is clear that the bureaucratic form does not assure equal opportunity, nor is it a barrier to equal opportunity.

The principle of being impersonal promises, and largely delivers, objectivity, equality of treatment and consistency.

The problem is that neither customers nor employees are satisfied by being equally *treated*. They really want to be equally *satisfied*. And, equal satisfaction requires treating some people differently.

Johnston's law:

If you treat everyone the same, what varies is satisfaction. To achieve equal satisfaction, you must vary treatment.

Example: Fixing the work hours, e.g., 9 to 5 or 8 to 4 will please some employees and dissatisfy others. "Flextime" varies the working hours and allows for equal satisfaction.

Example: A fixed set of benefits ensures variable satisfaction. A "cafeteria" approach to benefits, allowing each person to choose according to their individual situation and need, offers a better chance of uniform satisfaction.

The bureaucratic principle of an *up-focused mission* promises that the entire organization will focus on pleasing those who own or control the organization. This, however, comes at the expense of a focus on customer satisfaction or product quality.

If the success of the organization depends on satisfying the customer, or delivering a quality product, then the mission needs to be focused on customer satisfaction or product quality.

Some elaboration on the idea of an in-focused or an up-focused mission.

An up-focused mission is one that serves some group outside of the organization, such as the board of directors, the stockholders, the legislature, or the regulators.

For example, one group of electric utility executives chose "maintaining or increasing the dividends payable to stockholders" as their primary mission. In other words, their organization exists to serve its stockholders. I suspect when the franchise was originally granted, giving the organization an exclusive right to provide a certain geography with electric service, the customers and the politicians would have thought the primary mission of the organization was to serve the community and its customers. Certainly, all interested parties were willing to have the organization provide a fair return to its investors, but few customers would agree with the premise that the organization exists to serve its stockholders.

In-focused missions are missions that aim at achieving some internal goal that will benefit the organization itself, rather than benefit customers or stockholders—other than indirectly.

For example, some organizations define their mission in terms of growth, or market share, or profitability. Growth, market share and profits are reasonable "tactical" or "strategic" objectives, but they make very poor missions.

The mission defines what the organization is in business to do, and how it intends to measure itself.

Peter Drucker is perhaps the best known of the many business scholars who have pointed out that the only legitimate mission of any business organization is to attract and satisfy customers.

Throughout this book you will find recommendations that organizations replace in-focused or up-focused missions with a customer-focused mission.

A customer-focused mission will be expressed in terms of the customer, and will be measured in terms of direct or indirect feedback from customers.

Here are some examples of customer focused missions:

Kaset International's mission is: "To help organizations achieve extraordinary customer relations."

Profit, growth and market share are all important by-products of executing the mission well, but they aren't the goal, they are only by-products.

A customer-focused mission for a bank might be: "To create and maintain customer banking relationships that our customers feel are personally and financially rewarding."

If this bank achieves its mission, then growth is assured, and because loyal customers are less rate sensitive, the probability of good profits is high. But, it is important to notice that profits and growth are by-products, and the mission is customer satisfaction.

One vital difference between an in-focused mission and a customer-focused mission is that a customer-focused mission has the power to energize, motivate and guide ALL employees in the organization, whereas only a few people in a bank would jump out of bed each morning eager to get to work to increase "profit" or to assure "growth." In-focused missions create organizations with two missions, where top management is interested in achieving the mission (profit, growth, market share), and the mission of the rest of the organization is to attract and keep enough customers so that the real mission can be realized.

Customer-focused missions have the power to guide, energize and motivate employees at all levels of the organization. This makes it possible to have an organization that is totally aligned on the mission, and avoid the bureaucratic result of having split missions, or worse yet, apathetic alignment on an up-focused mission.

Some organizations attempt to have both a customer-focused mission and an in-focused mission—in other words, a "split" mission.

To clarify this idea, imagine a line that you could draw through the traditional pyramid shape of a given bureaucratic organization.

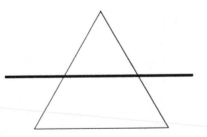

Below the line are the people who do the day-to-day work of the enterprise. Let's use an electric utility as an example. The people below the line are the linemen, meter readers, power plant operators, customer service clerks, etc. If these people don't show up for work, the actual job of producing, delivering and collecting for electrical power would somehow be compromised, and the difference might, in some way, impact a customer.

Above the line are the top executives, the senior managers, and the financial, legal, planning and staff people who have little if anything to do with the day-to-day work of delivering electricity.

If the people above the line don't show up for work, customers would not be impacted.

In organizations that attempt to have a split mission, the mission of the group above the line is either up-focused or in-focused. The people above the line are all there to support the CEO in satisfying the stockholders, the board of directors, the rate setting agencies, etc.

Below the line, the mission is "nominally" different. The people below the line are charged with the mission of satisfying the customer. The published mission of the organization might be something like: our mission is to provide safe, reliable, electric service that satisfies customers.

Over time, however, the two separate missions virtually always merge into one; the one adopted by people at the top of the organization.

Because the enterprise is organized using a formal "hierarchical" structure, the amount of pay, influence, control and power are all determined by the "level" of job you have with the organization.

Because "level" is so important, people entering the organization at the bottom keep a close eye on what it takes to climb the "ladder" and rise in the organization. They quickly notice something that seems to be a constant in organizations organized using the bureaucratic form—the people above the line are striving to achieve an in-focused, or up-focused goal—let's say that goal is "profit." They further notice that a key test for whether or not people within the organization are chosen to be promoted "above the line" is whether they are "management kind of people." A key question people above the line ask themselves is, "Does this person have the right kind of attitude?"

People quickly notice that the "right kind of attitude" is the attitude manifested by the people above the line.

So, here we have the crux of the problem. In theory, people below the line should be focused on customer satisfaction. They should be flexible, responsive and caring enough to dazzle customers. Yet, the people who get chosen to go "above the line" are people whose thinking and attitudes match those of the people above the line, which is focused on profit—not customer satisfaction.

So, what do you think happens? People below the line, with the important goal of rising above the line, align their attitudes and goals with the folks above the line. So, you have a person below the line who is paid to be customer focused, but has been seduced into being in-focused.

Gradually, the result of this transformation is that virtually all of the people below the line adopt the mission of the people above the line, and the whole organization reluctantly, and without commitment, aligns around an in-focused or up-focused mission. The only people really focused on customer satisfaction are those who don't understand the politics of the situation.

To summarize this observation:

a. If top management's mission is up-focused or in-focused, then eventually the entire organization will adopt the up-focused or in-focused mission.

b. In order to achieve a customer-focused, or quality-focused mission, top management must adopt and live out the customer-focused or quality-focused mission.

Some elaboration on Parkinson's law.

I have observed something else in support of Parkinson and Parkinson's law. Parkinson observed that the group above the line has a predisposition to grow at an alarming rate. Parkinson, with tongue only partly in cheek, estimated this rate of growth in the staff above the line at approximately six percent compounded annually.

Parkinson further observed that growth above the line has absolutely no correlation with what is happening below the line, so it almost doesn't matter whether the sample electric company is in a growth market or a static market—the head count above the line grows in either case.

Inspired by Parkinson, and with some wonderful opportunities to observe large organizations at work, I noticed something else that seems universal, but I haven't seen pointed out by other authors. I've noticed that the people above the line tend to think that good management involves keeping the staff "below the line" as small as possible.

So, we have, in the evolving bureaucratic organization, two simultaneous forces at work. We have Parkinson's law assuring that the number of people "above the line" will grow. And we have strong management pressure on the staff "below the line" to shrink. This produces, in the fully mature bureaucracy, the outcome I describe as **top heavy, bottom lean.**

The number of people below the line may not actually shrink, but relative to the growth of the organization, it is considered good "productivity" if the staff below the line grows at a lesser rate than the growth of the revenues of the organization.

Particularly in a service industry, the effect of top-heavy bottom-lean is to cause service to gradually deteriorate until the organization performs very poorly in terms of customer satisfaction.

Some elaborations on Johnston's Law and the issue of diversity in the workplace.

What is the issue of "workplace diversity" all about?

In the introduction to Marilyn Loden and Judy B. Rosener's book, *Workforce America!* (subtitled: *Managing employee diversity as a vital resource*), they say:

"...organizations throughout America are facing an extraordinary new challenge—unlike any they have confronted in the past...few U.S. institutions seem adequately prepared today to deal effectively with this momentous change—the increasing cultural diversity of the American workforce. By cultural diversity, we are referring primarily to differences in age, ethnic heritage, gender, physical ability/qualities, race and sexual/affectional orientation."

The issue of cultural diversity is currently "hot." Books are being written, seminars are being held—what is it all about?

With apologies for blatant oversimplification, I think it means that people don't want to be all treated the same. I think it means that they want their differences to be respected. I think it is another example of Johnston's Law: if you treat everybody the same, you get varying levels of satisfaction.

The bureaucratic form promises equal treatment for everybody. However, people don't want to be treated equally, they want to be equally satisfied.

What women are saying is, "Respect our differences. Don't expect us to act and be exactly like men." People of color are saying, "Respect our differences. Don't expect us to act and be exactly like Caucasians." Older people are saying, "respect our differences. Don't expect us to act and be exactly like younger people."

What bureaucracies are saying is, "We want to be fair. We want to treat everybody alike. We want to treat everybody the way that we want to be treated, and we will expect everyone to live up to our expectations."

What bureaucracies are failing to notice is that in many cases the expectations they are using are standards that are normally found in white, older, male, Anglo-Saxon Protestants (or whatever makeup reflects the highest-level people in that particular organization).

Johnston's law fits the issue of workplace diversity: "To achieve equal satisfaction, you must vary treatment." In order to satisfy them, you need to do what your co-workers want. You need to examine and understand the many differences that exist between them. You need to respect their differences. You need to vary your treatment and expectations to gain the advantage that exists in diversity.

Summary

• This chapter has examined the theory of the bureaucratic form and has shown that it does not live up to its promises. Instead of efficient and smooth-working organizations, the bureaucratic form produces organizations that are top heavy and bottom lean, where risks are avoided, responsibilities are evaded, people become in-focused, customers and employees are treated like numbers, procedures become rigid and fixed and customers do not feel well served.

Chapter Five

What evidence is there that the negative by-products of bureaucracy are caused by using the bureaucratic organizing form?

Preview

This chapter outlines the observations that led the author to link the negative symptoms we informally call "bureaucracy" with the use of the bureaucratic organizing form.

In thirty-one years of examining organizations from the inside out, I can summarize my experience this way:

A. The "stuff" we call bureaucracy shows up in every organization that uses bureaucracy as the organizing model.

B. The more stringently the organization applies these organizing principles:

   1. hierarchy

   2. rules

   3. impersonality

   4. organizing into functional units

   5. an in-focused (or up-focused) mission

   6. hiring based on technical qualifications

   the more striking the evidence of bureaucracy.

C. Most employees tend to blame their bureaucracy on senior management. Yet their senior managers are victimized by the negative by-products just as the rest of the employees are. And, senior managers are the people I find to be most eager to find a cure for bureaucracy. Think about it! If the symptoms are so common that we can list them in this book, then those symptoms can't be blamed on any given set of managers.

D. When organizations decide to change their mission, or any of the basic organizing principles, the negative stuff diminishes. This has been so commonly observed that some people think that "customer focus" campaigns, by themselves, are a cure for bureaucracy.

E. Organizations that use organizing models other than the bureaucratic model have fewer and sometimes none of the bureaucratic by-products.

   The Japanese, for example, inadvertently have moderated several principles of bureaucracy, and demonstrated how effectively a modified bureaucratic form can compete with bureaucratic enterprises.

Even the most successful of the Japanese companies still have a long way to go to eliminate bureaucracy; however, typical successful Japanese organizations have:

- **missions directed at customer focused quality,** supported by clear strategies and long term time perspectives that serve to align managers and employees.

- a very strong and clear-cut "hierarchy"—but **some of the worst effects of hierarchy are moderated by a cultural endorsement of consensus seeking.**

- **moderated the principle of "specialization" by bringing different specialities together in project teams,** and by having a customer-focused mission, specialists are induced to subordinate their craft to the larger mission.

A tenable hypothesis: Businesses in North America and Europe who seek to compete with successful Japanese organizations have the opportunity to catch them or pass them up by replacing their bureaucracies with organizational forms even more effective than the modified bureaucratic form.

Chapter Six

The mission-driven organization—a better organizing form

Preview

This chapter introduces a completely different organizing form as an alternative to the bureaucratic form. By examining the "mission-driven" form, you will learn that there are viable alternatives to the traditional bureaucratic form.

The bureaucratic organizing model is so pervasive that many executives are unable to even imagine another way of organizing an enterprise.

There are many possible variations of the bureaucratic organizing form that an enterprise may use. Many organizations have achieved success simply by changing one of the underlying principles. These have been amply documented by various people.

- *The Service Edge*, by Ron Zemke and Dick Schaaf, documents the 101 best service companies, and Tom Peters has co-written *In Search of Excellence* and *A Passion For Excellence*, in which he reported multiple observations of organizations that have modified or replaced at least one of the basic principles of the bureaucratic form.

(As you read any of these books, notice how the best performing companies have converted to a customer-focused mission, or flattened out to reduce hierarchy, or become sensitive to the human needs of their customers, or converted to multi-functional work teams, etc.)

Start-up organizations could bypass the bureaucratic model from the beginning.

As this is being written, in the early 1990s, the Republics (once part of the Soviet Union), Cuba, the nations of eastern Europe, and soon perhaps China, will all need their citizens to start enterprises from the ground up. These new enterprises will be faced with competing in an increasingly global economy dominated by huge, well-capitalized organizations.

If those new organizations adopt the bureaucracy organizing model used by the mature and established competition, they may forever trail behind. If, on the other hand, the new organizations choose more productive organizing paradigms, they have the opportunity to catch and pass the huge bureaucracies that currently dominate international commerce.

The mission driven model is offered as a model that start-up organizations can use. In this model, the energy of the employees—focused by the mission, strategy and vision of the organization—can make up for the start-up capital they may lack. I believe that the creative new organizations forming today have the opportunity to attract global capital as they take the concepts of product quality and customer satisfaction to new heights.

Existing bureaucratic organizations can use this model as of one of the alternatives to bureaucracy that they might seek.

In many ways, it is more challenging to be part of an existing bureaucratic organization that seeks to transform itself into a global competitor than it is to start a new enterprise from scratch.

To achieve significant change requires a change in mission, at a minimum. It is traumatic for an established bureaucratic organization to change its mission. There is an immediate impact on the culture. Employees will be cynical, and people will be slow to adopt the desired change.

In later chapters, we discuss the special challenges of transforming existing bureaucratic organizations. For all but a few existing organizations, the "mission-driven" model presented below will be too extreme a change. Most existing organizations will likely settle for some part of this vision. For those few that have the capacity, the freedom and the leadership to strive to become "world class" organizations, I offer the mission-driven model as an ideal.

The "mission-driven" model

The mission-driven organization will have a customer focused mission.

The most powerful principle in the bureaucratic organizing form is the mission. The bureaucratic form assumes a mission that defines the organization's purpose as serving itself or its owners or sponsors.

Mission-driven organizations will choose a mission that is focused on *the customer*. The specific mission will depend on the nature of the products or services that the organization intends to provide to its customers.

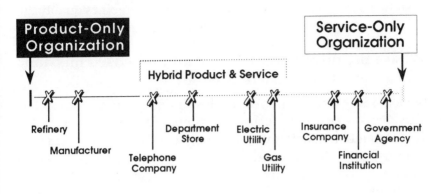

©1990 Kaset International, from the article, "Steps to Achieving"

The above continuum illustrates that organizations range from product-only organizations to service-only organizations, and many organizations offer both.

Product-based organizations might define their mission in terms of customer satisfying product quality.

For manufacturers, whose customer loyalty will be most deeply influenced by the customer's perception of *product* quality, the mission of the organization might be to produce the highest possible product quality.

Service-based organizations will aim for extraordinary customer service.

For organizations like banks and insurance companies, whose customer satisfaction depends on the organization's policies, practices and procedures—in combination with the human interactions of its people—the mission could be to deliver service that pleases, delights or dazzles customers.

Hybrid organizations will make it their mission to achieve customer dazzling service and satisfying product or service quality.

Hybrid organizations, whose customer's loyalty depends not only on the quality of the product or service that they offer, but also the

customer service, must choose a mission that combines quality and
service—always with the focus on achieving customer satisfaction.

What's the difference between an in-focused mission and a customer-focused mission?

Sometimes, executives from bureaucratic organizations "think" they
already have customer-focused missions. They point to their mission statement, which says something like, "Customers come first
with us," and they wave their internal campaign literature pro-
claiming, "We're nothing without our customers," or "Quality is
our future."

The difference between an in-focused mission and a customer-focused mission shows up best in the trenches. When you truly have a
customer-focused mission, then virtually all employees will
"strongly agree" with the statement, "The number one priority with
both employees and management is satisfying the customer" (or
product quality).

If you have an in-focused mission (masquerading as a customer-
focused mission), then employees will be ambivalent, or they will
strongly agree with a statement like: "While we talk a lot about
quality or customer satisfaction, the most important thing to management is profits" (or cost savings, or market share, or avoiding
commission complaints).

The primary measures that define organizational success will be based on customer satisfaction, rather than in-focused measures like profit or funding.

If your mission is quality, then you will measure customers' perceptions of *quality* and judge your organization's performance on the *results*. If your mission is customer satisfaction, then you will measure *customer satisfaction* and judge your organization's performance on those scores. You will prove the truth of the cliche, "What you measure is what you get."

"Mission-driven" organizations will use "hierarchy" in a new way.

The concept of "hierarchy" has both useful and damaging elements. Mission-driven organizations will keep the useful elements and abandon the rest. The key ideas will be to minimize the number of layers of management, and to push decision-making authority to the lowest practical level. Each remaining level of management will have a unique role to play. Higher levels will not be used for controlling lower levels or to make decisions that can effectively be made closer to the customer or product.

Senior management will define the mission, procure the capital, set the goals, articulate the vision and strategy, and interface with external stakeholders.

In bureaucracies, only senior managers really need to understand the mission, have a vision and implement the strategy. This is because senior managers are going to make all of the key decisions and establish the rules under which everyone else will operate.

In mission-driven organizations, on the other hand, the employees closest to the product or customer will be trained and empowered to make key decisions affecting product quality and customer satisfaction. In order for front-line people to make sound decisions, they must understand and embrace the mission, be clear about the vision, understand the strategy and be committed to the goals.

The role of senior management changes. Instead of making all of the key decisions, they will set and communicate the mission, strategy, vision and goals. Their primary role will be to focus and shape the decision-making of people who may be far removed from senior management.

In the mission-driven organization, senior management removes itself from decisions on operating issues and does its best to buffer the rest of the organization from the "upstairs" stakeholders (board of directors, stockholders, regulators, legislators, etc.).

Middle management will define the teams, allocate resources, remove obstacles and support mission achievement.

Middle management's job is to establish action teams (or strategic business units) organized by customer segment or product, remove obstacles to the team's success, monitor customer satisfaction, and lead the cheers when the teams make progress toward realizing the vision. Even the middle management level will delegate the key strategic and tactical decisions to the action teams closest to the product or customers.

The balance of the organization will organize into cross-functional action teams to achieve the mission by defining and then continuously improving quality, service, or both.

The bulk of the organization will form into teams responsible for serving individual products or market segments. They will take responsibility for achieving their part of the overall mission by creating extraordinary quality, service, or both (as dictated by the product or customer segment they serve).

Rather than the bureaucratic strategy of keeping the product or service constant through rigid application of the idea of "consistency," they will instead strive for "continuous improvement" (understanding that they will treat some customers differently to achieve consistently high levels of satisfaction).

Continuous improvement is an ongoing process which continually refines the product or service in order to achieve better and better quality, service, or both. Customer satisfaction with quality/ service is continuously monitored to provide feedback to the action teams about customer needs, expectations and perceptions. The customer feedback is used to drive change to ensure that the product/service achieves higher and higher customer satisfaction scores.

Status, prestige and financial rewards will accrue to those who contribute the most toward achieving the mission.

In a mission driven organization—unlike bureaucracy, where the rewards go to the leaders and managers—the rewards go to the individuals or teams that are contributing most to delighting customers. Managers will earn recognition for doing their share in establishing optimal missions, strategies and goals, and for their effectiveness in creating and communicating visions that can be realized by the action teams. But, the bulk of the rewards and recognition will accrue to the teams who achieve the mission and realize the vision.

The measures that drive action as well as rewards and recognition will be customer satisfaction measurements.

Mission-driven organizations will drive change and improvement from customer satisfaction measurements. Bureaucratic organizations use internal measures to drive change. Measurements of profits or expenses relative to budget or revenues are typical of the kinds of measures used to stimulate change in the bureaucratic organization. These are in-focused measures and are aligned with the in-focused mission. In contrast, mission-driven organizations will use customer satisfaction feedback to drive internal change.

Mission-driven organizations will also have a different strategy for employee recognition. Unlike bureaucracies, where *managers* select those who will be recognized and rewarded, the mission-driven organization will use *internal and external customer satisfaction* measurements as the primary determinant of who gets recognized.

Management assessments and possibly peer assessments may be added to the customer satisfaction measures, but mission achievement will be the primary input to recognition and rewards.

To recap, hierarchy will be used to establish the mission, and set the initial goals, the strategy and the original vision. Hierarchy will play a role in monitoring the team results to ensure teams are aligning with the mission vision, strategy and goals.

As the teams are empowered to achieve the mission, the teams may take on the responsibility of adjusting the strategy, setting their own long-term goals, and refining the vision in order to better achieve the mission.

When teams are so effective that they can be held totally responsible for their own goals, strategies and vision, they can be said to be "self directed."

Once teams are "self directed," the traditional bureaucratic organizing form's concept of hierarchy will have been totally displaced by the mission-driven concept of empowered teams.

Guidelines and other levels of empowerment will largely replace rules.

In bureaucracies, people are empowered to make decisions based on their level within the organizational hierarchy. In mission-driven organizations, people are empowered to make decisions based on their experience, skill, training or capability, rather than their level. This means that an individual in an entry-level position can gradually become more and more empowered to make decisions without being forced to rise in organizational level.

Kaset International's training program, "Managing Extraordinary Service," identified five levels of empowerment.

	Not Serious	Fairly Serious	Very Serious
High	**Level 1** Totally Empowered	**Level 2** Post-Action	**Level 3** Guidelines
Medium	**Level 2** Post-Action	**Level 3** Guidelines	**Level 4** Pre-Action
Low	**Level 3** Guidelines	**Level 4** Pre-Action	**Level 5** Not Empowered

Person/Team (vertical axis)

← **Seriousness of Consequence** →

No empowerment—in situations where the potential negative outcome of a poor decision is of great consequence to the organization; or in situations in which the individual lacks the experience, skill, training, or capability to make good decisions. At this level of empowerment, the individual either gets management to decide or follows specific rules, thus eliminating individual decision-making. This is the normal level at which people operate in bureaucratic organizations.

Pre-action empowerment—in situations where the individual is learning, practicing or proving his/her ability to make good mission-driven decisions, or where the consequences of a mistake are more than the organization is willing to risk. In these situations, the individual comes to an "empowerer" with his/her own decision before actually implementing the decision. This allows opportunity for confirmation or corrective coaching.

Empowerment with guidelines—in situations where the individual is entrusted to make mission-achieving decisions within guidelines. As long at the individual stays within the guidelines, the individual is empowered to make decisions that, in other organizations, might be reserved for supervisors or managers. This level of empowerment makes it possible for front line people to make mission-achieving decisions, thereby delighting customers, without having to chase up the line to get managerial approval.

Post-action empowerment—in situations where the individual has the experience, skill, or training to make good decisions, or for situations where a poor decision (relative to the mission) is not of the most serious consequence. At this level, the individual proceeds to make decisions, but periodically goes over them—after they are made—with an empowerer as an opportunity for coaching and further development.

Total empowerment—in individuals who are experienced, skilled, trained or have proven capable of making sound mission-achieving decisions. At this level of empowerment, individuals are empowered to make decisions that go outside of guidelines without further approval or post-action review.

To summarize the principle of empowerment, notice that:

- The mission-driven organization deals with levels of empowerment, rather than levels of management. In very flat organizations, where authority levels are limited or non-existent, individuals still learn and achieve personal growth through empowerment. Individual accomplishment and experience contribute to growth in empowerment, related to the mission. This contrasts sharply with the bureaucratic form, which typically links growth (in organizational levels) to support of internal objectives.

- In the bureaucratic form, achieving higher levels generally takes people farther and farther away from the customer or the product (the trenches). The mission-driven model gives individuals the ability to grow, learn, achieve more responsibility, earn higher income and stay close to the customer or product—where the action is.

Business needs will be balanced with human needs.

The mission-driven form actively encourages balancing business needs with the human needs of both customers and employees. This is in stark contrast with the bureaucratic form, which seeks to treat all customers the same, whatever their individual needs, and encourages employees to "leave their personal lives at the door."

Research with customers and employees shows that loyalty and satisfaction can only be achieved when the organization attends to the human as well as the business needs of people. Customer relations experts suggest that the human and business needs of customers be integrated into each transaction. The chart on the next page (the human-business model) represents the idea graphically. The chart suggests that interactions with customers (internal or external) weave a path between the consideration of the human needs and consideration of the business needs of the transaction.

Human-Business Model

In Any Interaction

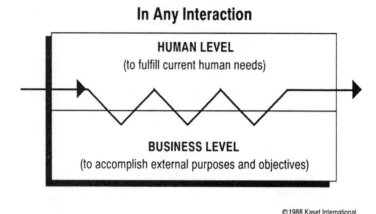

©1988 Kaset International

Mission achievement will depend on meeting the human needs of customers.

Whether achieving the mission is dependent on product quality or customer service, or both, mission-driven organizations will attend to the customers' personal and human needs as well as their business needs.

Phase one of the quality revolution was producing products with zero defects. Phase two is producing products that meet the human needs of the customer. Premium automobile designers today are considerate of how a car "feels," how it "sounds" and how it expresses "caring" for the user.

Organizations whose mission is to achieve extraordinary customer service are learning that customer loyalty is most strongly influenced by human issues such as how much the organization seems to "care" about its customers. Achieving extraordinary customer service requires treating each customer in the way that the customer wants and needs to be treated. The extraordinary flexibility and fluidity required of the mission-driven organization are implemented by empowered people and flexible policies, practices and procedures.

The mission-driven organization will be considerate of the human needs of its employees as well as its customers.

The mission driven organization depends on its employees for the achievement of its mission. (This contrasts with the bureaucratic form, which depends primarily on management for the achievement of its in-focused mission.) Because of this difference, for the organization to achieve its mission, employees must be committed to the mission and loyal to the organization.

Employee loyalty, like customer loyalty, depends on the organization attending to the human needs of the individual. This reality can be stated both positively and negatively. If the organization doesn't "care" about its employees, it will be difficult to get the employees to "care" about its customers. Conversely, an organization that "cares" about its employees will have employees who are more likely to "care" about its customers.

In summary, mission-driven organizations will take great pains to attend to the individual human needs of each of their customers, and to the individual human needs of each of their employees. This contrasts sharply with the "purposely impersonal" principle that underlies the bureaucratic organizing model.

Multi-functional teams will replace specialization by job function.

The mission-driven organization will seek to eliminate functional "walls" or "boundaries" that must be crossed to achieve the mission.* The idea is to put every function that will be needed by a business unit on the same team.

The goal is to be sure that every resource or skill that the team will need to continuously improve service, quality, or both, is available on the team—without having to cross any organizational boundary. This organizational principle may appear to produce internal inefficiencies, but, because it is customer focused, it is designed to optimize customer satisfaction rather than to achieve the in-focused goal of minimizing front-line staffing levels.

Cross functional teaming is in stark contrast to the bureaucratic form, which groups people by the work they do or the training they've had, with the intent of creating efficiencies that benefit the organization. This is another example of the difference between what is optimized in an in-focused mission and what is optimized in a customer-focused organization.

*General Electric's widely respected CEO, Jack Welch, has been frequently quoted in the popular business press about what he calls "a boundaryless company."

Hiring will be based on both human and business skills.

Mission-driven organizations will seek to hire for such human attributes as "attitude," "desire," "commitment" and "caring," as well as the necessary business skills. The organization is concerned with the human needs of its customers and its employees. Both customers and employees will be affected by the human facets of new employees joining the organization. Mission-driven organizations cannot allow their mission to be sabotaged by employees who think the world "owes" them a living, or whose interpersonal skills make it intolerable to work around them. This is not to say that mission-driven organizations will be arbitrary or discriminatory in their hiring. It is clearly possible to be non-discriminatory in hiring, and still give strong consideration to human factors that support achieving the mission.

Again, this is in stark contrast to the bureaucratic form, which purposely excludes consideration of human factors in hiring. The bureaucratic model may succeed in reducing discrimination by rigidly testing only business attributes, but the impact of employees with terrible work attitudes and abominable interpersonal skills is damaging to both fellow employees and customers.

Job security will be a function of mission achievement.

The mission-driven organization will provide job security linked to the individual's contribution to mission achievement. Individuals who contribute to mission achievement will be highly valued and will earn job security as a by-product. Individuals who act directly or indirectly as barriers to mission achievement will have little job security. The mission-driven organization will base performance assessments on a range of inputs, from teammates, teamleaders, and, where possible, from direct or indirect customer feedback.

The bureaucratic form allows for virtually total job security in some cases (e.g., tenure) and in other cases offers substantial protection against arbitrary dismissal (e.g., civil service). It has never been shown that providing absolute job security produces better learning in universities or better public service from government workers. On the other hand, this is another clear piece of evidence that achieving success within a bureaucracy has little to do with serving those the bureaucracy is chartered to serve.

Some conclusions.

The ideal form of the "mission-driven" organization is almost directly antithetical to the bureaucracy organizing form. (Each of the organizing principles seems to be almost the opposite of the other form.)

It is not necessary to adopt every element of the "mission-driven" form to experience a huge relief from bureaucracy. Notice, however, that all of the principles of the mission-driven form are harmonious and aligned. And, all of the components of the bureaucratic form are harmonious and aligned.

When you change only one of the principles of bureaucracy, you gain great relief from the symptoms we call bureaucracy, but at the same time, you create tension and misalignment. Gradually, each of the other organizing principles has to adjust to regain alignment with the piece you change, or else the principle you change has to return to its original state to resolve the tension.

The organization will feel most secure and unconflicted when all of the principles of the bureaucracy form or the mission-driven form are adopted. When you adopt only some of the principles, you can expect that some organizational tensions will arise. You must then be prepared to accommodate and work around the tensions.

Summary

• The principles of the mission-driven organizing form are virtually the opposite of the bureaucratic organizing form.

The "mission-driven" model will:

   a. be driven by a customer-focused mission, based on extraordinary product quality, or customer service that exceeds customer expectations, or both.

   b. use hierarchy in a new way.

      1. Senior management will define the mission, procure the capital, set the goals, articulate the vision and strategy, and interface with external stakeholders.

      2. Middle management will define the work teams, allocate resources, remove obstacles, and support mission achievement.

      3. Non-managers will organize into cross-functional teams to achieve the mission.

   c. use guidelines and other levels of empowerment to largely replace rules.

   d. balance business needs with human needs for customers and employees.

   e. use cross-functional teams to replace work units organized by function.

   f. hire employees based on human skills as well as business skills.

   g. base job security on success in mission achievement.

Chapter Seven

How to de-bureaucratize

Preview

This section is written for readers who are part of a mature bureaucratic organization that wants to de-bureaucratize. This chapter aims to introduce the process and give you an overview so you can see past the detailed steps and understand the overall concept.

Each organization is different. Each must find its own way through the process. Each will have a different goal. Each will have a different sense of commitment. Each will have a different culture. Each will have different barriers and different advantages.

After observing hundreds of organizations attempting to transform themselves in one way or another, I offer the following observations that are gained from the hard won experience of those organizations.

- Be aware that your goal has to be more than just to de-bureaucratize. Your goal is to replace bureaucracy with a more desirable state. So, the change process will be to move "toward" something better, rather than to "get rid of" the existing state. You de-bureaucratize as a by-product of achieving "quality" or "extraordinary service" or some other customer-focused goal.

- You fool yourself if you think you can reduce bureaucracy by substituting one in-focused set of goals for another in-focused set of goals. In other words, you don't de-bureaucratize by mounting a campaign for better profits, or lower costs, or higher dividends. These are examples of the kinds of goals that led your organization to becoming bureaucratic in the first place.

- Senior management commitment is the key determinant of success. If you have it, and can maintain it for long enough, your change effort can succeed. If you only have a little commitment, or if you lose the commitment you have, you'll be likely to quickly revert back to the present state.

- If your senior management team is clear in its understanding of what is required, and it has a strong commitment, it can choose an ambitious goal and achieve it. If senior management is unclear about what is required, or if each of the senior managers has a different view of how ambitious the change should be, then it is best to choose a more modest goal.

- Middle managers, because of their existing goals and measures, are the biggest barrier to achieving success. To succeed, middle managers must play important roles in the change process, and new customer-focused goals and performance management measures must be substituted for the existing in-focused set.

- Achieving the desired goal state will take longer than senior management expects. *Achieving the goal state is a process*—not a project. It doesn't have an end, and it will never be finished.

- A "shadow" organization is a "must" if you hope to achieve even modest long-term change. The "shadow" organization is an informal organization, superimposed upon the existing organization, consisting of teams with names like steering committee, task force, action teams, etc. The shadow organization will spearhead the change effort and will be made up of the people who will facilitate and manage the change.

  Without a shadow organization, the bureaucracy in the existing organization will, in spite of good intentions, unwittingly sabotage and ultimately destroy the change effort. And, it may take years to discover that the change effort has failed.

- The most critical period is the middle phase, when you are partway through the change. You have part of the organization living in the "old world" and part of it living in the "new world." If you don't understand that the feeling of "one foot in each world" is normal, you may give up your gains and snap back into bureaucracy.

- You are likely starting from a position where you are "top-heavy" and "bottom-lean." If it's not too late, resist the temptation to "downsize" and instead redeploy your redundant middle managers. Redeploy them to the shadow organization, or to the field organization where they can help solve the leanness problem and fill in for managers who need to be retrained in their new roles.

- Keeping the redundant managers will be more expensive than replacing them with new lower-level employees. On the other hand, you'll gain by keeping the managers' experience and by building a more loyal team. Be clear, however, that managers who are unwilling or unable to work effectively at a level closer to the customer will not be allowed to impede the change effort.

Overview of the process of how to de-bureaucratize.

The following is designed to digest the chapters that follow. It is not important that you understand each point, but it may be valuable for you to have a sense of the overall process.

Get professional help, but do the work yourselves.

The most successful organizations are those who used outsiders to guide them at the beginning, but kept control of the change process and developed their own internal people as consultants and trainers and scorekeepers.

Choose continuous improvement as a strategy.

Continuous improvement transfers the responsibility for customer satisfaction to the people nearest the customer. Continuous improvement requires a shadow organization, teams of front-line people trained as problem solvers, and customer feedback to drive change. Using continuous improvement, rather than traditional managerial problem solving, multiplies the amount of change, enrolls and motivates front-line people, and by its nature, serves to de-bureaucratize the organization.

Make an assessment of your present situation.

Make an initial assessment of your existing state. Add up your advantages and take note of the barriers. Assess your present customer satisfaction. Assess your employee attitudes. Assess the current amount of bureaucracy and its negative by-products. Assess your readiness for change, and assess the amount and quality of senior management commitment.

Choose the optimal "goal state."

Based on your assessment and senior management commitment, choose a modest, moderate, or ambitious goal state. What would you like the organization to become in the future? How will it look to customers? How will it be to work there? How will it compare to other organizations of your type?

Set up a "shadow organization" to manage the change.

Based on your goal state and your assessment, set up the optimal "shadow organization." You will seek the right mix of steering committees, task forces and action teams to achieve your goal. Your choice of goal state will determine whether the shadow organization is permanent or temporary, and whether it is staffed with people who work on teams part time or full time. Your goal state will determine whether the teams are aligned with the existing functional organization, or purposely cross functional.

Begin collecting customer feedback to drive the change.

Begin the process of collecting continuous streams of feedback from customers that will drive the change effort. Collect feedback relating to the "moments of truth" that most greatly impact the customer's relationship with your organization. Collect "qualitive" feedback, with small sample sizes. Action teams, working to improve quality or service, will use the feedback to drive the changes they make as they continuously improve service, quality, or both. The customer feedback will also be used as a baseline of current customer satisfaction. The baseline will be useful to monitor changes as customer satisfaction is improved.

Train your front-line people to work in teams and to implement continuous improvement.

Train them to solve problems using the most powerful problem-solving strategies available. Train them to prioritize the process to be improved, or the moment of truth to be managed, based on its impact on your relationship with your customers. Empower the teams to continuously improve your quality, service, or both.

Do what it takes to gain the support of your entire management team.

Teach your managers the principles of bureaucracy—what fosters it, and what they can do to minimize it. Teach them how to manage using continuous improvement, rather than traditional management problem solving. Teach them how to operate on and with shadow organization teams, such as task forces, steering committees and action teams. Teach them how to manage in an empowered environment.

Do what it takes to gain the support of your non-management people.

Convince your non-management people that this isn't just another "program." Help them understand the process, their role in it, and what is in it for them. Ask for their feedback, use their feedback and keep your people well-informed.

Manage the change in the culture that will result from the change effort.

Understand the changes in beliefs that will mark the transition from a bureaucratic organizing form to a mission-driven form. Communicate those belief changes to all employees so they can support the new culture instead of fighting it.

How you will know you are there.

You'll know that you've achieved your goal by the feedback you get from your customers and from your employees. You'll know that you've achieved your goal by what your people are doing, and how different it is from what they are doing currently. You'll know by your position in your industry or marketplace. You'll know by the pride and satisfaction you and your fellow employees have in your organization.

Summary

• This chapter summarizes the steps that an organization could take to move away from the bureaucratic organizing model and toward a better model. These steps are:

   a. get professional guidance, but do the work yourselves.

   b. use continuous improvement as a strategy to replace the traditional "top-down" management-driven, problem-solving strategy.

   c. begin with an assessment of your present situation.

   d. choose the optimal goal state.

   e. set up a "shadow organization" to manage the change.

   f. use customer feedback to drive change and measure progress.

   g. train your people to work in teams and use advanced techniques for solving problems.

   h. gain the support of your management team, and teach them how to work in the world of empowerment and teams.

   i. earn the support of your non-management people.

   j. manage the change in the culture that must take place to enable organizational change.

   k. create a vision of what your organization will be like when you've achieved your chosen goal state.

Chapter Eight

Get professional help, but do the job yourselves

Preview

This chapter elaborates on my recommendation that you bring in professionals to help you plan any significant change effort. I further suggest that you select advisors who will transfer their knowledge to your people, so your own employees can implement the changes and "own" the end result.

The principles of organizational change and the principles of culture change are well understood today by organizational development specialists. I encourage you to use them to guide your change effort.

I have witnessed numerous change efforts that failed because the organization didn't have the expertise to plan and manage the effort on their own, and they didn't seek professional guidance. On the other hand, I have seen change efforts fail because the outside consultants were generalists and didn't have experience with planning and guiding change efforts. So, outside consultants are certainly no guarantee of success.

As you seek help, check with the existing customers of any consulting organization you are considering. Ask the references how successful the change effort is, and whether the result lives up to what the consultant led them to expect. Also, look specifically for proof that the external consultants have created independence in the referenced organization, rather than the more traditional dependence that some consultants create by hoarding the knowledge. I suggest you seek multiple references. Ask the consultants for their entire customer list, and you do the choosing about which customers to call.

It is important to have your own internal consultants and change agents, but keep them within the shadow organization.

The most successful change efforts I have seen are those in which the outside consultants transferred their knowledge and expertise to inside consultants who became responsible for implementation.

By having outside consultants plan and guide the effort, you avoid getting caught up in the internal power politics that typically occur when internal consultants are used to plan the change effort.

By having inside consultants implement the change effort—from the political neutrality of the shadow organization—the organization is taking responsibility for its own fate and takes ownership of the transformation.

By placing the internal consultants and facilitators in the "shadow" organization of steering committees, task forces and action teams, you have your change agents where the changes are taking place, and they are out of the political quicksand that typically exists within the functional organization.

Find a supplier who can provide a full spectrum of products and services to support your transformation. Otherwise, you'll have to select a consulting group, a training company, and a customer satisfaction feedback supplier. Then *you'll* have to make them all fit together.

■ *A personal story—Back in 1984, a large, regulated, organization was being deregulated and restructured, and a new division was formed whose strategy was to become "customer focused." They felt they needed to convert from a "regulated mentality" to a "market-driven" mentality. They selected my company to be their training supplier; they selected a consulting company to be their consultants; and they selected a measurement company to help them track their progress.*

When I asked that we be introduced to the consulting company, so that we could design our training programs to "fit" the overall plan, we were turned down. This is a wonderful example of bureaucracy in action. We were turned down because the person we were dealing with only dealt with the training aspects, and somebody else was responsible for dealing with the consultants. When our contact went to the VP with our request, it was turned down. The VP wasn't willing to pay the consulting firm to consult with the training firm. As he put it, "I'm not going to pay for one outside firm to consult with another outside firm. We picked them because they supposedly know their business. Let them do what we paid them to do."

I'm unable to report on the success of the venture, because another reorganization followed a year later, and the division totally disappeared. However, I learned from that experience that organizations seeking to transform themselves need a single supplier that can supply the entire system of support: consulting to define the plan, training to support the plan and customer feedback to track progress.

Summary

• If you plan a significant change effort, you'll need expertise in organizational change, in driving change through customer feedback or process measurements, and in training your people to handle changed roles.

• Unless you want to become the integrator of multiple suppliers' specialties, select a support organization that can help you with your plan, the measurements you'll need to drive change, and the training your people will need.

• Unless you want to be dependent on your vendor for the success of your organizational change, insist that your people be trained in each of the roles necessary to achieve the desired change. Bureaucracies are accustomed to dependency on outside consultants. As you leave the bureaucratic form behind, the organization you seek may be one that "owns" the ability to continuously change to improve itself.

Chapter Nine

"Continuous improvement" as a primary strategy for your organization

Preview

In this chapter you'll learn about the power of continuous improvement and how it differs from the traditional management problem-solving approach. Find out why I say that "continuous improvement" is the most important change in organizational design in the last century.

What is continuous improvement, and how does it compare to traditional management problem solving?

Perhaps once a century, an idea comes along that is so powerful and so compelling that it can be said to "revolutionize" industry.

Alvin Toffler, in his 1990 book *Power Shift*, concludes we are beyond the industrial revolution and have entered the "knowledge" revolution. We are all intellectually aware that we who manage, now manage brains more than brawn. Yet, we aren't as aware that our management styles and strategies are more attuned to the industrial revolution than the knowledge revolution, and to the management of brawn more than brains.

Every thoughtful observer has noticed that something revolutionary has been happening in Japan, as their industrial organizations have come to dominate the world of manufacturing. Yet, only recently, have our eyes been opened to the real secret of the Japanese miracle. We all noticed the extraordinary "quality" of the goods being produced. In fact, many of us actually thought that "quality" was the secret. Yet, thousands of European, Canadian, and U.S. firms have installed "quality," and are still waiting for the miracle to hit them.

What many observers have now noticed is that the secret doesn't lie in the concepts of "quality." The secret lies in the "continuous improvement" of quality.

As a matter of fact, you could "continuously improve" service just as easily as you continuously improve quality. Or, you could "continuously improve" quality and service.

"Continuous improvement" is a way of managing. And, it is a way of managing that is perfect for "managing brains" in this era of post industrial revolution.

Let's see how "continuous improvement" contrasts with traditional management problem solving left over from the industrial revolution.

What does it take to achieve continuous improvement?

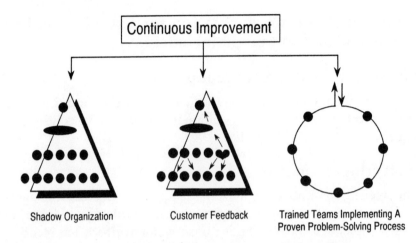

Shadow Organization | Customer Feedback | Trained Teams Implementing A Proven Problem-Solving Process

To install continuous improvement requires three things:

1. You need to organize a shadow organization that is right for your organization.

2. You'll need to continuously collect customer feedback and use that feedback to drive improvement.

3. You'll need people to work on problem-solving teams who are trained to work in teams, trained in quality/service skills, trained in effective problem-solving processes, and committed to customer satisfaction.

1. Shadow Organization

What is a shadow organization, and why do you need one?

A shadow organization is an "informal" organization, superimposed upon a formal organization.

Organizations form "shadow" organizations to get work done that would be difficult to do within the formal organization. Other terms that are sometimes used are "informal" organizations, or "parallel" organizations.

If you are used to terms like "steering committee" or "task force" or "action teams," then you are most likely using some form of shadow organization now.

A typical shadow organization for a service quality improvement effort might include:

The senior management group

Senior management decides on the goal of the effort and the scope of the effort, and creates the mandate that will achieve continuous improvement of service quality.

A steering committee

The steering committee might be made up of some senior managers and some upper-middle managers, and their role would be to actually implement the continuous improvement effort. The steering committee will form the task forces and empower them and monitor their success until the desired goal state is achieved.

Task forces

Task forces would be made up of cross functional teams of middle managers and professional staff who would form and monitor the action teams that will actually do the work of continuously improving service quality. Task forces will support the action teams with responsive approvals, assignments and links to the functional organization so that the shadow organization and functional organization work smoothly together.

Action teams

The action teams will be made up of front-line people who will actually implement continuous improvement of service quality. The action teams will apply proven problem-solving strategies to fix both internal and external customer problems, and add service enhancements to provide exceptional service to internal and external customers.

Links to the functional organization

Managers throughout all of the functional units in the functional organization will be assigned to participate in task forces in the "shadow" organization. Their purpose will be to ensure that the two organizations stay aligned.

Benefits of installing a "shadow" organization.

Managers in bureaucratic organizations tend to be very busy already, which means they can't easily find the time to "drive" organizational change. Managers can, however, "monitor" the change process; the shadow organization puts managers in the role of *monitoring*, as opposed to *doing*.

The shadow organization can have a flat hierarchy, and can empower people to make decisions based on skills and experience rather than organization level. The teams can be cross functional so they can cut through the departmental boundary walls that tie bureaucratic organizations in knots.

The shadow organization can be sharply focused. Its mission is to change the way the organization functions.

When driving a lot of change, the organization needs to be able to respond quickly. The shadow organization can do that, whereas the functional organization is slow to respond or adapt. (A more complete explanation of shadow organizations can be found in Appendix II.)

2. Customer Feedback

You'll need a continuous flow of customer inputs to drive improvement, and continuous customer feedback for monitoring thereafter.

You'll need to be able to determine customer expectations.

Action teams will need to know what customers expect in order to define the standards that will satisfy them and the service enhancers that will please or delight them.

You'll want a baseline on your present state of service quality so you can track changes.

Action teams will need to know the present level of customer satisfaction with existing service and quality in order to measure the results of the changes that they implement.

You'll want continuous feedback from customers so you can determine that the changes you make are working.

As the teams make changes in any component of customer service, they'll need continuous feedback from customers to validate their assumptions and to ensure that they are truly improving service, quality, or both.

You'll want to measure the customer satisfaction your internal service units are providing to internal customers.

Action teams will be improving service quality to internal customers. Partly you want this because good internal service is often linked to the quality and service you can give your external customer. You also want to give *employees* good service because you need them to be loyal, caring and committed to the organization so you can count on them to implement the continuous improvement process with commitment—even passion.

You'll want to benchmark competitors or other organizations that are the "best in class" in terms of the mission-aligned activities that you do.

If you are striving for extraordinary service, quality, or both, you'll want to bypass the "not invented here" mentality that so often limits bureaucratic organizations, and look for positive models inside and outside of your industry.

Most importantly, you'll want to have your new measurements actually "drive" change through the organization, and take precedence over existing in-focused measurements.

Quality and service improvements both are driven by customer feedback. You may find that in-focused measurements are currently driving employees' actions that are hurting service or quality.

Example: We discovered that telephone customer service reps in one Northeastern utility company were hanging up on time-consuming customers to meet their daily call quotas.

The shadow organization will be prepared to surface existing measurements that may be driving undesirable actions and to reduce or eliminate the influence those measures have. This will assure that customer inputs and feedback will be the dominant drivers of action and change throughout the organization.

You'll also need to change the way that customer satisfaction feedback is dealt with inside the organization. In most bureaucratic organizations, customer dissatisfaction is "bad news," and sometimes the cure is to shoot the messenger. To achieve continuous improvement, the frame of reference needs to change. You will want to start viewing customer dissatisfaction as something "valuable," because it drives improvement. You will want to begin to view customer feedback as "diagnostic," rather than as a measure of performance. This is an important culture change to make, because if you keep shooting the messenger, pretty quickly you'll only get good news, and improvement becomes impossible.

3. Committed and Trained Employees

You need employees who are trained, willing and able to produce satisfying core service and dazzling customer service.

Organization and customer feedback will make continuous improvement possible, but success depends on employees who are committed to service quality improvement, trained to work in teams, and trained to apply their problem-solving skills to those customer situations that are most important to your customers.

You'll need to train your employees so they can participate in the task forces and action teams that will produce the continuous improvement.

In bureaucratic organizations, the amount of training and development an employee gets usually is based on their level. Managers make the key decisions and "get things done," so managers get the training. When you are seeking to de-bureaucratize, and empower lower-level employees to solve service and quality problems, you'll need to give those employees far more training than bureaucracies are used to giving to lower-level people. One of the barriers to organizational change efforts is the "traditional" allocation of training by level. Senior managers can find themselves stuck in the old bureaucratic way of thinking and resist investing in the growth and development of what they think of as lower-level people.

Another misperception that is common in bureaucratic organizations is thinking that working in teams is something that everyone "knows" how to do, and that problem solving is something that, at least, all "managers" intuitively know how to do. Well, this turns out not to be true. Problem solving is a process that almost anyone can be taught to do, and that few know how to do very well unless they've been trained. Teamwork improves incredibly once people have been trained in the processes that make teams work effectively together.

Summary

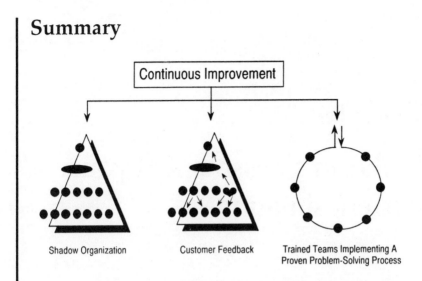

| Shadow Organization | Customer Feedback | Trained Teams Implementing A Proven Problem-Solving Process |

- It is the interaction of shadow organization, customer feedback data and people trained in the continuous improvement process that combine to achieve continuous improvement.

In chapters that follow, the shadow organization, customer feedback and training in continuous improvement will be explained in more depth.

Chapter Ten

Make an assessment of your current situation

Preview

This chapter invites you to make an assessment of your existing situation and the commitment available to you from stakeholders and senior management—before you begin a change effort. You'll learn some of the things you'll want to know about your existing organization before you begin your change effort.

I suggest that you begin a de-bureaucratizing change effort by making an assessment of your present situation. It is helpful to be clear about the problems that you have, the barriers to change that you face and the strengths that will make your task easier.

Which of the problems that normally impact bureaucracies do you face?

The debilitating effects of bureaucracy are so great that it is common to find severe problems in product quality, service quality, or both.

It is also very common to find senior management insulated from the seriousness of these issues, because of the bureaucratic tendency of each level of management to report positive results upwards, and because of the typical lack of regular feedback from customers.

Quality of your products or core service?

You'll want to know the present level of customer satisfaction with your core products or services. How well do your products meet customer expectations? How committed are your employees to quality or service? How important are quality or service to your management team, compared to the more usual in-focused types of measurements that typically drive managers?

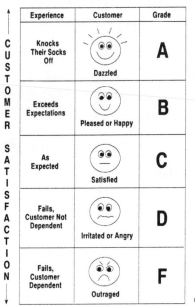

Experience	Customer	Grade
Knocks Their Socks Off	Dazzled	A
Exceeds Expectations	Pleased or Happy	B
As Expected	Satisfied	C
Fails, Customer Not Dependent	Irritated or Angry	D
Fails, Customer Dependent	Outraged	F

CUSTOMER SATISFACTION

©1991 Kaset International

Customer service that doesn't dazzle?

Is customer service an important part of the satisfaction level of your customers? If so, does it satisfy customers? Does it please customers? Does it make customers happy? Does customer loyalty mean very much to your organization? Is your customer service building customer loyalty?

Employees who are stressed out, immobilized, disaffected, or all three?

What is the current stress level of your employees? Is it within healthy ranges or is it excessive? Do your employees feel empowered and able to flex the system to produce quality or satisfy customers? Or, do they feel immobilized by rules and bureaucratic barriers to achieving the mission? Do your employees feel like part of the team or do they feel alienated?

A lack of innovation?

Is innovation important to your future success? How satisfied are you with your organization's ability to innovate with new products and services? Is your organization one step behind the market place or the industry? Or are you leading the way?

Inability to keep up with a rapid rate of change in your industry?

How rapid is the rate of change in your industry? Are you keeping up? Are you leading the way?

How serious are the consequences if you don't do anything?

What are the risks to the organization? What are the risks to employees, past, present and future? What are the risks to other stakeholders?

Do you have competition? How tough is it?

How competitive is your industry? How competitive is your niche? How do you stand relative to your competitors? What are the prospects and forecasts of your relative competitive position in the future?

Do you face de-regulation, re-regulation or privatization?

If you are regulated, or an agency of government, do you face de-regulation or privitization? If you've been de-regulated, do you face re-regulation?

How much commitment do you have within your senior management team?

Perhaps one of the most important things to discover in an assessment is the amount of commitment that you have within your senior management team. How committed is your CEO? Are senior managers in agreement about the need for change?

Would your stakeholders give you the freedom you need to make an unfettered choice?

Who are your critical stakeholders? How much support is there for change? How possible will it be to gain stakeholder agreement with a commitment to de-bureaucratizing or to improving customer satisfaction? How long can you count on that support? What could cause the support to diminish?

When you have completed an informal or formal assessment of your present situation, you are prepared to choose an appropriate goal state. What do you want your future state to be?

Summary

• An assessment is an excellent beginning to a change effort. You'll want to assess your present competitive situation, your present strengths, your present weaknesses, the state of your employee group, the consequences of change and the consequences of not changing. You'll need to be clear about the extent of management and stakeholder commitment to change. When you have a clear assessment, and a clear goal state, it is simple to identify the gaps and focus your change effort on the specific issues that your organization faces.

Chapter Eleven

Choose the appropriate goal state

Preview

This chapter clarifies the task of choosing what you want your organization to be, instead of being bureaucratic. You'll find that the amount of stakeholder and management commitment will determine how ambitious your change effort can be. You'll learn that your choice of goal determines the strategy that you choose.

Why do you need a goal state?

Everyone agrees that you can't stop being one thing without becoming another. In other words, if you change, you become something different.

So, if you want to eliminate the suffocating effects of bureaucracy, you need to decide what you want to become instead. If you don't substitute a new desired state, then your people will only know what you *don't* want, and they won't know what *to do* instead. So, you risk chaos by focusing on "stopping" something without replacing it with a coherent, thoughtfully chosen goal.

Notice the title of this book, *Busting Bureaucracy*. The title suggests that you give up bureaucracy, but doesn't suggest an alternative.

I've chosen to stick with *Busting Bureaucracy* because I want the book to appeal to organizations mired in bureaucracy who might pick a range of choices of alternative goals. I didn't want to limit this book to just one of the alternative goals.

So far, I've talked about three different missions you could choose that would be great alternatives to being in-focused and bureaucratic. I've described the choices as being focused on service or quality or both—service quality.

In this section, I will add the concept of "depth" or "scope" to the idea of mission. In other words, you could decide to focus on "quality" and do it for awhile, just until quality became acceptable. Or, you could focus on quality and make it the primary ongoing focus of your organization. Or, you could focus on quality and do "anything it takes" to achieve it.

"One shoe" doesn't fit all—when it comes to organizational change.

Every organization is unique. Every management team has its own unique makeup. Executives mean a variety of different things when they use terms such as "customer sensitive" or "customer focused" or "customer driven."

Even though two different organizations might say the same thing, e.g., "We want to become customer driven," I've found that they might have vastly different ideas about what being customer driven means.

It's not that these organizations were attempting to be unclear. It's clear that even between fellow executives they can have vastly different ideas in mind when they say, "We want to become customer focused."

I've found that it is very important to make the desired goal very clear. The clearer you are about your goal, the more likely it will be that your managers and your people will be clear about what they need to do to achieve the goal.

Being clear about your goal will help you make good decisions about the strategy and processes you use to change your organization.

First, I'll describe three different goal states. I've given each of them a different name. One I've called "customer sensitive," one is called "customer focused" and one is called "customer driven." I intend to make meaningful distinctions between these three different states.

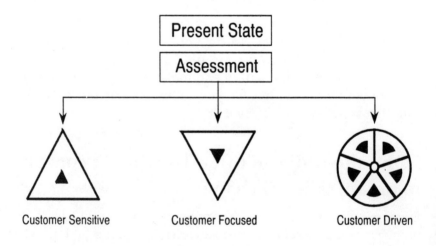

1. The Customer-Sensitive Goal State

The same traditional organization, but more "customer sensitive."

The "customer-sensitive" goal state is for organizations that really have no compelling reason to move away from their existing organizational form. They may want to improve customer service, or service quality, but they are not willing, or may not be able to change the organization's fundamental mission or make significant changes in the way the organization is organized.

For example, think of a government agency, created by legislators responsible for serving the legislature, whose mission is defined by the legislature. Even though the agency may want to become "customer focused" or even "customer driven," they lack the freedom to make substantial changes in their mission or organizing model.

For another example, think of a bank, purchased by a holding company, responsible to the holding company, with a mission defined by the holding company. Even though that bank's management team may want to make the bank "customer focused," or even "customer driven," they may lack the freedom to choose their own mission or organizing model.

You choose this goal state when you want to continue using the bureaucratic form of organizing, but want to improve service quality and reduce the negative effects of bureaucracy produced by using the organizational form.

Review of the bureaucratic form:

1. **In-focused or up-focused mission**—The mission of the organization is to serve stakeholders above (e.g., stockholders, regulators or legislators). Or, the mission is in-focused, serving the needs of the organization itself (e.g., profits, funding, growth, market share, etc.).

2. **Hierarchy**—Each level controls the levels below it, and is controlled by the levels above it. The power to make decisions is based on level.

3. **Rules**—Each level controls the levels below by creating rules. Each level is governed by rules created by levels above it.

4. **Impersonal**—The idea of being purposely impersonal is to wring the human element and personal judgment out of any dealings with employees or customers, with the goal of treating everyone equally.

5. **Organized by function or specialty**—People within the organization are organized by the work they do or the function they serve. The goal is efficiency and optimization of function.

6. **Hiring based on technical qualifications**—Hiring without regard to individual differences or subjective issues, (e.g., personality, teamwork, etc.).

You choose this goal if you want the freedom to move on to new goals and new programs once you have improved service, quality, or both, and as a by-product also reduced the negative effects of bureaucracy.

Many organizations don't have the stakeholder commitment sufficient to make "service quality" improvement the driving force in their organization. At least some of the senior executives may see de-bureaucratization or service quality improvement as "the program of the year," and want to be able to move on to other priorities once service quality is satisfactory.

When you have improved customer satisfaction and reduced the damaging effects of bureaucracy, you may want to return to business as usual.

For some organizations, innovations like "continuous improvement" are too big a step. Continuous improvement requires rethinking management roles and the traditional roles of employees. While the organization may be willing to employ such a novel approach for some period of time, the private hope of the senior executives may be to return to "business as usual" once the service or quality problems are fixed.

2. Customer-focused goal state

This second goal state is called "customer focused" because it changes the mission—one of the six major principles of the bureaucratic organizing form.

You can choose this option if you have agreement from stakeholders or senior management that you want to change from an in-focused or up-focused mission to a customer-focused mission.

In effect, you are willing to turn the traditional pyramid upside down to indicate that the customer is "on top." This suggests that the entire organization is aligned in support of satisfying the customer.

- you are willing to trust that if you do what is right for the customer, that profits, growth, market share, rate increases, funding increases and other internal needs will be natural by-products.

- you have reasonable confidence that you can align the entire organization around the goal of pleasing, delighting or dazzling customers.

- you believe that operating the business to serve customers is the best strategy for the long term, and you are willing to make a long term commitment to putting the customers' interests first.

- you do not have a consensus to change the other organizing principles for the enterprise. So, you plan to continue organizing hierarchically, managing by rules, being impersonal with employees (though not with customers), and organizing by function or specialty.

3. The "customer-driven" goal state

This book uses the term "customer driven" to suggest a goal in which the organization is willing to do "whatever it takes" to achieve extraordinary customer relations.

You can choose this option if:

- you have stakeholder agreement to adopt a customer focused mission.

- your senior executives and outside stakeholders are willing to trust that profits, growth, market share or funding will be natural by-products.

- you have confidence that you can align the entire organization around a customer-focused mission.

- you also have enough support and commitment to *reorganize* the entire enterprise, if necessary, to maximize customer loyalty (or willingness to continue being served).

- you seek to create an extraordinary organization as well as extraordinary customer relations.

- you are willing to shift from being functionally organized to an organization utilizing multi-functional teams wherever that would better allow the organization to serve customers.

- you are willing to use employee empowerment, along with guidelines—instead of rules—whenever empowerment will better achieve the organization's mission.

- you are willing to give up impersonal treatment of employees and customers wherever doing so would build customer or employee loyalty to the organization and its mission.

- you are willing to shift away from a many-leveled hierarchy to a *fairly* flat organization with the fewest practical levels, with decision authority based on experience, training, skill and closeness to the customer.

Summary

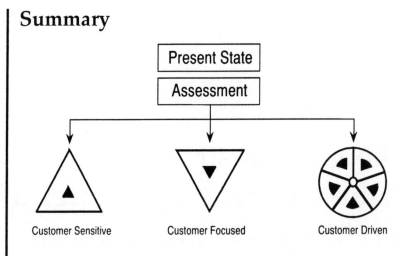

| Customer Sensitive | Customer Focused | Customer Driven |

Customer Sensitive

• Maintain your present organizational form, bring your core service quality up to customer expectations, and deliver better than expected customer service. As a by-product of these improvements reduce the amount of "bureaucracy" that your customers and the people in your organization experience.

Customer Focused

• Convert to a customer-focused mission, produce extraordinary customer relations, and, except for the mission, maintain the other characteristics of the bureaucratic organizing model (hierarchy, rules, impersonality, organizing by function and hiring based on technical qualification).

Customer Driven

• Willingly change any of the principles of the organizational form necessary to achieve an extraordinary organization, the goal being extraordinary customer relations, as well as an extraordinary organization.

Chapter Twelve

Choose your strategy for de-bureaucratizing through a service quality improvement effort

Preview

In this section we'll bring the two ideas together: the idea of goal states, and the idea of continuous improvement, in order to see how the selection of a goal state would influence your strategy as you implement continuous improvement.

1. Strategies for achieving a "customer-sensitive" goal state.

In this goal state, the idea is to maintain the traditional organization but to gain the benefits of reduced bureaucracy and increased customer satisfaction that come from implementing a quality or service improvement program.

You may not have enough stakeholder or management commitment to undertake a continuous improvement process. You may be forced to limit your program to training for front-line employees, supervisors and managers.

Many organizations that suffer the effects of excessive bureaucracy will not have enough management commitment to install a continuous improvement system with a shadow organization, customer satisfaction measurement, and training in problem solving. These organizations will be limited to the use of traditional change strategies such as employee, supervisory and management training.

These organizations could choose to teach managers and front-line people about bureaucracy, and aim directly at reducing the negative effects of bureaucracy. Or, these organizations might use training focused on service or quality improvement to gain the de-bureaucratizing by-products that service quality improvement produces.

It is important to note that training, by itself, can make a significant difference in service quality. Many, if not most, organizations use training as the primary approach to improving service quality. Training has proven to be a powerful change tool.

If you have more than a minimum amount of management commitment, you may go beyond training and install new customer feedback systems for tracking customer satisfaction.

You may have enough commitment or resources to introduce continuous customer feedback to drive the change process. This will make it possible to form action teams and make product or service quality improvements, even though there may be no formal shadow organization of task forces and steering committee to support the teams.

Most organizations that choose the "customer-sensitive" goal state elect to have an outside organization do their customer satisfaction tracking rather than disrupt their present organization by creating a new functional department.

When senior managers view service quality improvement as less than a permanent commitment, they may resist forming a permanent new functional unit responsible for collecting and disseminating customer inputs and feedback. As long as the primary mission is still up-focused or in-focused, then the most important measurements will be those that drive the organization currently. As a result, customer satisfaction feedback is not seen as being very important and thus can be left in the hands of outsiders.

If your organization has sufficient commitment, you may choose to implement a continuous improvement system, combining training, customer satisfaction measurement and people organized into teams in some form of "shadow" organization to continuously improve service quality.

Organizations with a "customer-sensitive" goal state will probably choose to fill the steering committee and task forces with managers and executives who are assigned these duties in addition to their existing jobs.

By making the continuous improvement process an added job, management can be fairly certain that when service quality has improved, the managers involved will easily return to business as usual, and they will not have to undo any permanent organizational changes.

The organization may not want to make action teams a permanent way of working in the organization. They may limit the number of action teams created, and allow action teams to die out when they have brought service quality to an acceptable level and the most blatant negative aspects of bureaucracy have been moderated.

2. If your goal is to become "customer focused."

In this goal state, you intend to permanently change from an in-focused mission to a customer-focused mission, leaving the rest of the traditional bureaucratic form's organizing principles unchanged.

You will almost certainly want a continuous improvement system that will work long into the future to please and delight customers with ever-improving service quality.

You will want to consider staffing the task forces and steering committee with some or all full-time people.

You will want to give thought to staffing the shadow organization with your best and brightest "fast track" managers.

You may want to introduce teams as a permanent way of working, and will consider training all of your people in teaming skills whether they are part of the shadow organization in multi-functional teams or whether they remain in the functional organization in functional units.

Hopefully, you will plan ahead to the time when the shadow organization and the underlying functional organization will be in conflict with each other and create organizational tensions. Planning and awareness can moderate the negative stresses.

You will want to fund and staff your own internal capacity for assessing customer expectations and tracking customer satisfaction. Customer satisfaction measurements will begin to "drive" the organization and will be too important to delegate to outsiders.

3. If your goal is to be "customer driven."

In this goal state, you will build around the process of continuous improvement.

You will want to build your own internal capability to collect customer feedback. Over time, you will gradually add more and more customer feedback measures until all of the major systems of the organization are driven by customer inputs and feedback.

You will want to gradually reduce the effect and influence that in-focused measurements have on the organization. You will maintain sufficient control over processes and collect enough in-focused measurements (e.g., budgets, productivity, etc.) to ensure that your in-focused goals can continue to be met. The difference is that the in-focused measures will no longer be the primary drivers for the organization or the key measures used in performance management.

Customer-driven organizations have very different cultures from traditional bureaucratic organizations. You will want to ensure that the shadow organization adopts the desired customer-driven culture and passes it on to each person as they transition from the bureaucratic culture, through the shadow organization, to a place in the newly created, customer-driven organization.

You will want every employee in the organization to learn team processes, to learn service quality improvement, and to be clear about the vision for the organization you seek to create.

You will want to ensure that the resulting, customer-driven organization is empowered, non-hierarchical, concerned with the human needs of employees, and that decision authority goes with competence, experience, training and skill rather than organizational level.

You will want to ensure that guidelines replace rules (other than those dictated by laws, society or regulators), and that people are empowered to go outside of the guidelines when they stand in the way of achieving the mission.

With everything planned from the beginning, and with the customer-driven goal state clearly in view, you will want to gradually redeploy people from the existing functional units, through the transitional shadow organization, into the newly designed customer-driven organization.

Summary

• To de-bureaucratize and to improve customer satisfaction, you will need to change the focus of your organization from in-focused to out-focused. The goal state you choose will determine whether you intend a permanent change or a temporary change. The basic nature of your organization will determine whether you will convert from being in-focused to being focused on quality, service, or both.

• The degree of commitment you have from senior management and your stakeholders will determine the extent or magnitude of the goal state you can choose.

• If you have limited commitment, it is prudent to set a limited goal. You might choose the goal state called "customer sensitive."

• If you have moderate commitment, you might choose the goal state called "customer focused."

• If you have very strong commitment from stakeholders and senior management, you can choose the most ambitious goal state, being "customer driven."

• Your choice of focus (service, quality, or both) and your choice of goal state (customer sensitive, focused, or driven) will dictate your strategy in designing the optimal shadow organization to help you realize your goal.

(For more information on constructing a shadow organization and how a sample shadow organization might work, see Appendix II, entitled "The Shadow Organization.")

Chapter Thirteen

Collect the customer feedback you need to drive the desired organizational change

Preview

In this chapter you'll learn about new kinds of customer feedback that you may need to begin collecting in order to drive continuous improvement in your organization. You'll learn how continuous, qualitative, transactional customer feedback is different from traditional customer satisfaction data, and how your teams would use the new feedback to continuously improve quality, service, or both.

The customer feedback you may be getting now probably won't be enough.

In years of working with organizations that want to achieve better customer relations, I have yet to find one organization that *is* collecting the kind of customer information that they need to increase customer satisfaction.

From what I know of the successful Japanese organizations, I have yet to discover one organization that *isn't* gathering the customer feedback they need to satisfy customers.

This stark, almost unbelievable, contrast makes it reasonably safe for me to predict that your North American or European organization is probably not collecting the kind of customer information that is needed to improve quality, service, or both.

You may be getting no regular customer feedback, or next to none.

Many organizations that I've worked with personally have had no regular system of collecting feedback from customers. Others do a survey of their customers every two, three, or even five years. Those periodic surveys generally include some questions related to how satisfied the customers are.

What you collect currently is probably global and directed at senior management.

If you have any regular feedback from customers, it is likely to be a "global" type survey, with the report written for senior management.

I use the word "global" to describe the kind of survey that samples all customers' segments, in all geographic sections, and asks questions about a wide range of things. For example, a global survey might ask questions about the organization's advertising, its marketing, its people and its facilities, and it may also collect customer opinions about the industry, new innovations in the industry, etc. In a global survey, only a few questions are usually devoted to issues of customer satisfaction, and those are generally somewhat cursory. If your customer information is of the "global" survey type, then it is most likely contained in a report written for senior management. This is important to notice, because a report written for senior management seldom contains the level of detail that would be useful in identifying specific customer dissatisfaction issues, and would not be helpful to teams in your organization chartered to improve specific elements of quality, or customer service during specific "moments of truth" (transactions which have a high impact on customer satisfaction or loyalty).

What you have now may even show customer data in the best possible light.

I am sad to report that some of the customer survey reports I have examined were produced in such a way as to make customer satisfaction look as good as possible.

I am not saying that market researchers distort their research. I am simply reporting that some organizations find negative customer feedback so discomforting that they react to it by "shooting the messenger."

■ *In one case, which I will disguise somewhat to protect the embarrassed, I was shown three customer surveys, done over eight years, by three different market research firms.*

The earliest report contained good questions, a high-quality rating scale, and very poor customer satisfaction ratings. They fired the firm and buried the report. Senior management said that the report conflicted with constant feedback from the front lines that customers were very satisfied.

The second report contained good questions, a slightly less discriminating rating scale, but even more rigorous and professional survey protocol. The results were slightly higher, but still very low. The scores, however, were interwoven with narrative that made the low scores sound almost terrific. In this instance, the research was sound, but the interpretation was clearly designed to present bad news in the most favorable possible light. The second research firm wasn't told that it was fired, but they were never used again.

The third report contained leading questions and a primitive rating scale that would tend to distort the results. (A three-point scale, with the customer able to choose between very satisfied, somewhat satisfied, and terribly dissatisfied.)

*The customer only had three choices, and the top two were combined to give a score that showed that 82 percent of the customers were somewhat or very satisfied). Another way to view the same information (which was **not** written in the report), was that 65 percent of all customers were less than satisfied, and 18 percent of them were "terribly" dissatisfied.*

The report was glowing about the improvement in customer satisfaction that had been achieved since the prior reports, with no mention of the distortion caused by the questions or the rating scale.

Not surprisingly, the third report was well received by senior management, and was the first of the three reports that was circulated throughout the rest of management. As I understood it, the third market research firm was well thought of and would do any future research the company required.

I believe this story illustrates the concept that "if you shoot the messengers who bring bad news, you ensure that you'll only get good news." A steady diet of only "good news" can cause executives to become **"insulated."**

The information you get currently is almost certainly quantitative

Quantitative studies are used when large quantities of data are being collected. By making the survey quantitative, the results can be expressed in numbers. There is nothing wrong with quantitative measures; they provide a useful overall picture. Quantitative studies, however, do not produce the rich source of information about customer satisfaction, expectations, or loyalty that are produced by "qualitative" studies.

An example of qualitative information is a collection of comments by customers who might respond to the invitation to fill in the blank lines on a comment card. The problem with qualitative data is that it becomes overwhelming when it is collected in large quantities.

It is unwieldy, and it is very challenging to make good summary interpretations of qualitative feedback. So, when information is collected for senior management, qualitative data is seldom used—in North American or European bureaucracies. In Japan, however, and in the best quality and service organizations everywhere, qualitative information is used extensively.

For example, it has been become part of the lore in the hotel industry that Mr. Marriott of the Marriott corporation reads every customer comment card personally. This is very different from reading a single page summary of "highlights" from 1,500 comment cards. Two things happen when senior executives take a direct interest in "raw" qualitative data. First, the executives guarantee that they don't become insulated and "out of touch." Second, they give a powerful message to employees that it is important to satisfy each customer, and that making 75 percent of them satisfied isn't enough.

Existing customer feedback is probably not available to the people who need it to improve service or quality.

If you decide to de-bureaucratize by forming teams to improve quality, service, or both, the customer feedback you have currently is probably not specific enough to be useful, and it almost certainly isn't generally available to the non-management people that you would use to staff the shadow organization's action teams.

To drive organizational change using continuous improvement, you'll most likely need an entirely different kind of customer feedback.

I recommend that you collect mostly qualitative customer feedback, with just enough quantitative data to take a baseline and track progress.

When you use quantitative methods, the customer will typically be forced to answer the questions that *you* choose, using the answers that *you* make available in the boxes to check off. This can work out if you are smart enough to know exactly what questions to ask and include all of the possible answers for customers to choose from.

The reality is that researchers seldom ask the most interesting questions, and seldom put boxes in for every interesting answer the customer may want to give you.

Far more useful to the teams seeking to improve service quality is discovering what the customer thinks, wants, expects, or feels. If you ask the customer what he/she thinks is important, you'd better put in some blank lines for the customer to write on, or a person for the customer to talk to, because you'll never be able to predict all of the possible answers.

Customers literally "don't know" what makes them happy. Their predictions don't match their actions.

There is another small problem with gathering customers' expectations from quantitative studies. If you ask customers to tell you what factors will make them feel loyal to your organization, they'll tell you. They will list a bunch of factors, and they'll even weight them for you so you know the relative importance of each factor.

The problem is, customers consistently demonstrate that they "don't know" what will make them loyal. That is, they consistently make predictions that don't match their actions. They'll tell you that if you do X, Y and Z, they'll be loyal. But, when you ask customers why they left you, they'll say it's because of A, B or C.

So, we poor business people, charged with the job of figuring out what will make customers loyal or happy, eventually discover we have to choose. We have to choose between believing what customers *predict* will make them loyal, and what they report *actually* makes them feel loyal.

I suggest that you put more weight in what customers report than what they predict. I suggest you give more credit to their actions than to their words.

After years of working with customers from a broad range of organizations, I recommend that you study loyalty by asking customers to tell you why they are loyal to you or to someone else. When they demonstrate disloyalty by going to another supplier, I suggest you ask them why they left. And, I suggest you use the "critical incident" method of collecting customer feedback regarding satisfaction and loyalty.

Critical incident analysis is highly recommended for studying loyalty or satisfaction.

The critical incident methodology is a "qualitative" process, which yields stories or comments, rather than neat, easily scored check marks in boxes.

The questioner studying customer satisfaction for your organization would talk to customers, either over the phone or in customer intercepts at malls, or at your place of customer contact.

The most useful level of detail is the "transaction," or "moment of truth" if you are in a service organization, or a specific attribute of product performance if you are studying satisfaction with the quality of a product.

Global surveys may inquire about a customer's overall view of the organization, but you can't use that information to drive improvement. To drive service or quality improvement, you want your customer feedback to be specific to the "moment of truth" or product attribute an action team will be assigned to improve. So, as your people learn to collect critical-incident type feedback, it is important that they seek the feedback specifically about the transaction that they are working to improve.

Critical incidents provide feedback on expectations.

Your people will collect stories that illustrate why a customer is very satisfied or very dissatisfied. (Just being satisfied doesn't produce critical incident stories. Simply being satisfied isn't even very noticeable by the customer. Extremes in satisfaction yield the stories that explain how and why customers become loyal or disloyal to an organization).

If a customer reports an incident that dissatisfied them, the story will frequently point out what the customer expected and how the organization failed to meet their expectations.

When a customer reports an incident that dazzled them, they will frequently report that they didn't expect what they got and were happily surprised by it.

Critical incidents provide feedback on the impact of meeting or failing to meet customer expectations.

Critical incidents will illustrate the product or service elements that had an important impact on the customer's feelings of loyalty or disloyalty. If the customer reports being dazzled, then it becomes clear that the actions or product element that dazzled the customer is one with an important impact on customer satisfaction. Conversely, when a customer reports strong dissatisfaction, the critical incident that the customer describes will reveal a service or product element that has the power to strongly affect the customer's feelings about the organization.

Critical incidents show how to achieve loyalty.

My own qualitative research into customer loyalty and customer satisfaction shows that satisfaction with customer transactions and loyalty are very tightly linked.

As your people collect stories ("critical incidents"), and pay attention to what they tell you about customer expectations, impact and loyalty, they will identify the improvements that their teams can make in the product or service that will result in customer satisfaction and thus loyalty.

The feedback will need to be continuous so it can be used for baselining, tracking improvement and monitoring success.

In contrast to global studies, which tend to be annual or biannual, the feedback about transactions that your action teams need is continuous. First, they need to know the satisfaction level being provided as they begin to improve a moment of truth or product element.

Then, as they make changes in the way the moment of truth is managed or the product attribute, they need to gather feedback continuously, so they can see the effects of the changes they are making. When they drive the satisfaction level up to the desired high level, they can stop improving it, and begin to monitor satisfaction to ensure that it stays high.

After a moment of truth has been improved or a product element has been improved, the customer feedback needn't be continuous, but it still needs to be collected regularly to ensure the changes are still in place and working.

You'll have to learn to collect the information yourselves.

If your goal state is to become "customer sensitive," you might not want to set up an in-house function to collect customer feedback. But, for more ambitious goal states, it is a necessity that your organization learn how to continuously gather customer feedback—until the end of time.

First of all, outside researchers aren't set up for small run, continuous monitoring of small pieces like customer transactions. They are set up for large sample multi-question and periodic studies that are quantitative. So, if you want to do what really needs to be done, you'll have to train your people to do it themselves.

Secondly, the idea of collecting continuous feedback from customers isn't something that you will ever be finished doing. You'll have to do it as long as your organization aspires to high levels of quality or service. So, you might as well learn how to do it.

As you learn how to do it yourselves, you'll discover that it isn't difficult. It doesn't require people with degrees in market research or statistics. It just requires people who are willing to talk to customers and listen to their stories. And, it requires caring enough to sort through the stories to find out what really satisfies or dissatisfies customers.

You'll also discover that the act of surveying the customer, by itself, is an important "moment of truth." Most customers interpret a phone call or survey following a transaction as a demonstration of "caring" about customer satisfaction. Thus, the survey process itself shapes the customer's perception about the quality of your products or service.

You won't find the successful Japanese organizations doing without qualitative customer feedback.

Many of the successful Japanese organizations achieve their extraordinary customer satisfaction by getting close to their customers and paying great attention to the details of service and quality that impact customer loyalty. I don't know of any successful Japanese organizations that don't use customer feedback methods that are at least partially qualitative.

Summary

- To support continuous improvement of service, quality, or both, you'll need to supply your teams with continuous feedback from customers.

- The kind of feedback most useful to teams will be feedback specific to the moment of truth or product element that they are working to improve.

- The type of feedback most useful to teams will be qualitative feedback which includes the stories or "critical incidents" that contain information about customer expectations and satisfaction as well as the impact on the customer's loyalty.

- The quantities of feedback that teams need will tend to be very small so the volume of the data doesn't overwhelm the team's ability to absorb the messages.

- The teams need a continuous, small volume stream of feedback related to the moment of truth or product element they are improving. The data collected should be primarily qualitative with just enough quantitative data to track change. This will allow them to baseline satisfaction as they begin, track changes in satisfaction as they experiment with fixes, and monitor satisfaction on into the future to ensure the fixes continue to work.

Chapter Fourteen

Train every person in your organization whose role changes

Preview

This chapter presents employee training in new light. If you elect to de-bureaucratize, then everyone in the organization needs to learn how to work in the new way. Continuous improvement requires new skills and new behaviors of managers and team members.

Begin to view employees and managers in a new way.

In a bureaucratic organization, the one person responsible for the organization's success is the CEO. Right behind the CEO, in terms of responsibility for the success of the organization, are the senior managers, then middle managers, then supervisors, and finally (if they are given any credit at all), the non-managers.

This comfortable and orderly progression of "credit" for success, or "blame" for failure is reinforced throughout the social order, indeed, throughout the entire North American culture. So, if an organization succeeds, the CEO becomes the hero in the business literature. Conversely, if an organization fails, the CEO becomes the "scapegoat."

Until it is brought to their attention, few executives ever notice that this natural order of things is at the very root of the bureaucracy that immobilizes and suffocates the potential of the organization.

One reason it is so difficult for senior executives to give up the bureaucratic organizing form is that they fear giving up "control" by delegating authority and responsibility to people at lower levels in the organization. After all, they reason, "I'm going to be held responsible for the success of this organization, so I'd better control everything that I possibly can."

Even if the CEO is able to delegate total operational responsibility to the next level, the executive at that level faces the same feelings and fears of losing control by delegating.

The bottom line is simple. In de-bureaucratizing, or any other significant organizational change effort (e.g., "quality" or "customer satisfaction"), it is vital for senior managers to change they way they view the roles of managers and the people of the organization.

Senior management will still be important in terms of defining the mission, choosing the strategy, marshalling the necessary capital and other needed resources, and communicating the vision. In the new form of organization, their overall responsibility and their role changes relatively little, except in terms of making "rules" or constraining operational decisions. And, in addition, they must also define and communicate the mission, strategy and vision so that others can implement the strategy, carry out the mission and realize the vision. Senior managers need to stop believing that they can "control" the execution of the mission at or near the front lines. They will need to substitute empowerment (giving permission and protection) for control.

Middle managers will still play a vital role by organizing to carry out the strategy, allocating resources wisely, and doing their part to bring the vision to life. Their role changes from being "controlling" managers to becoming "coaches" and obstacle removers.

Functional staff people leave the "staff ghetto" and join the teams at the front lines so that action teams have access to their expertise without having to cross-departmental boundaries.

The most significant change occurs at the non-management level. The people at this level will organize into teams and change from being supervisor driven to being mission driven. The people in the teams will, by virtue of experience, capability and training, earn responsibilities and authority hardly dreamt of in the traditional bureaucracy. The teams will be responsible for some segment of customers, or some product, and will have the responsibility and authority to improve quality and service with the goal of maximizing customer satisfaction or loyalty.

Now, here is the "bottom line." To successfully de-bureaucratize, and not so incidentally achieve extraordinary quality or service for your customers, senior and middle management need to change the way they view "the employees." Using the bureaucratic model, it may have seemed normal that the "employees" could become alienated, hostile, underutilized, frustrated and overstressed.

To be a truly successful organization, you need to bring the employees "on board," and create one unified team of employees and management that are aligned around the same customer-focused mission.

"...and now, in harmony..."

What kind of view do you need to take of the employees? You need to see them as critical to the success of your mission. You need to see them as important and highly valued. You need to see them as people—real human beings whose attitudes and feelings of self-worth are critical to your success. You need to see them as your teammates.

When you see the non-managerial employees in this new way, then it becomes obvious that they are worth investing time and energy in.

Begin to think about training in a new way.

Historically, bureaucratic organizations have apportioned their training investment based on organizational level. This meant that (on a per capita basis) executives got the most training and development, middle managers somewhat less, supervisors less yet, and ordinary employees the least. To achieve organizational change, you will need to think differently about how you apportion your training investment.

To achieve the goal you select, you will want to use training and communications as change tools. The people whose role changes the most in the new organizational design need the most training. Organizations that are on the path to achieving the goal states that I have offered in this book are spending a greater per capita share of their training dollar on the people closest to the customer.

Share with all your people the mission, vision and strategy to build commitment to the change effort.

I don't recommend that you *start* the change effort by communicating the mission, strategy, and creating the vision. First of all, you probably aren't ready to do that, and until you have real clarity about the mission and strategy, I suggest you wait. Secondly, the idea of mission, strategy and vision are just *words* at the beginning of an organizational change effort. The approach I favor is called the "small splash" approach to announcing organizational change. This means you begin changing, and only talk about what you're doing, or what you've *actually done*, not about what you intend to do. Most organizations have had the "program of the year" for so long that most people will think this is just another one. And, if senior management falls short of persistence or commitment, it may turn out to be just that. But, if you are serious and committed, you will persist in the change effort to a point where people realize that this isn't just another program of the year.

Nonetheless, at some time in the early years of a transformational effort, the teams will be trained and in place and actively working on the continuous improvement of quality, service, or both. Once they've begun to understand their new role, and begin to believe that they are empowered, it's valuable to communicate the new, customer-focused mission. Since they are playing a key role in achieving the mission, they will need to understand the strategy that you have selected. And, so they can align themselves with what senior management wants, a clear, well-articulated vision is useful to help them see what it will look like, feel like, and be like when the vision is realized.

It doesn't hurt to tell people the new mission, the strategy and the vision at the beginning. So, if you've already begun a change effort and you began with the mission strategy and vision, don't worry. But, it is important that you intentionally go back and reinforce these communications after the changes are in place. Repetition won't hurt, and when the people have adopted a new way of thinking, they will be open to viewing the mission, strategy and vision with a different frame of reference.

Teach managers what they will need to know to manage in the new, less bureaucratic organization.

Managers' and supervisors' roles will change pretty dramatically. Unfortunately, training and communicating only play a small role in getting managers and supervisors to change the way they do their jobs.

It would be wonderful if you could just teach managers how you want them to manage differently in the future and have them walk off and behave differently. This can be done, but only in special cases. Training will work, by itself, if you have the luxury of being able to put the manager into a new work environment when the training is done. Hopefully, you will have people in place, working in the new way, with the new culture, in the new work environment.

Most managers, however, will return from their training to the same job, with the same role, and worst of all, with their existing goals and measurements.

If you are striving for a "customer-driven" goal state, you might have the freedom to recreate the organization anew, in a new physical space with people who have been plucked from the existing organization in small lots, trained in the new approach and installed into the new culture in an altered role.

Most organizations, however, will have less ambitious goals, and less freedom to toss everything up in the air and start over. If that is the case for you, then I suggest you don't count on training alone to help you transform the management team. I suggest you start with communicating the new vision and give enough training in the basics so they feel comfortable managing people who have the new skills. The real magic begins when you begin withdrawing existing goals and measurements that are almost certainly in-focused, and replacing them with customer-focused performance measurements.

By changing the rules of the organization's "game," changing the performance management system so they have different unit goals, and making sure the rewards go to those who excel at the new game, you will make your management team very interested in learning the new skills and attitudes they will need to win the new game. *It is a combination of structural changes and changes in the performance management system that will combine with training to produce the changes you seek.*

Teach people how to work effectively in teams, and teach the team members how to improve quality, service, or both, and empower them to do it continuously.

In some ways this is the easiest part of the task. If the nature of your organization dictates that you focus on quality improvement, the training to accomplish this is readily available from a variety of suppliers.

Another reason why training is one of the easiest parts of the change effort is that front-line people have a lot to gain. Their work life becomes much more interesting, varied and challenging as they are allowed to use the full range of talents that they bring to work. They gain in motivation because of the added elements of growth, responsibility, achievement and recognition that are added to their work. They gain pride in their organization as they see the positive effects of their work on customers.

It will not always be easy to "enroll" the front-line people in the effort. You may be starting with an alienated work force, perhaps unionized and maybe even openly hostile to anything management proposes. However, the experience of the many organizations already starting down the path of organizational change proves that it is possible—and getting easier all the time—as more employees and union managements become aware of changes other organizations are making.

Summary

• Senior managers need to re-examine the way they view the roles of managers and employees. The traditional "top down" view won't work when employee teams become responsible for problem solving, which has always been in management's domain.

• Managers accustomed to the hierarchical view of importance will need to understand that non-managerial employees are critical to achieving a customer-focused mission. In the new paradigm, employees will be viewed as teammates who are important and highly valued.

• Managers who allocate funding will need to rethink the way they allocate funding to training. They also will need to think differently about how that budget is apportioned between management training and training for people who will make up the continuous improvement teams.

• Everyone in the organization will eventually need to learn the mission and the strategy for achieving the mission. They also will need to understand and share the vision of what the organization can become. These needs can be considered communications or training. In either case, they are imperative if the people are to align around the mission.

• Anyone in a managerial role will need to learn how to coach, remove obstacles, and empower others. These skills must be trained. At the same time, the bureaucratic tools of disciplining and controlling can be extinguished, since they only produce conformity and submission, while smothering initiative.

• Working effectively in teams, and identifying root-causes in problem solving, are not common skills. All the evidence shows that they need to be taught. This is true whether you decide to remain as a bureaucracy or choose a new organizing model.

Chapter Fifteen

To become mission driven and to reduce or eliminate bureaucracy, you will need the support and participation of your entire management team

Preview

This chapter is written for senior and middle managers. It is offered as an outline of the training that you might give to your management team. They need to know what they are doing that is adding to the bureaucracy in your organization. They also need to know how to do their job without adding to the bureaucracy.

If you do nothing more than conduct training such as that outlined here, you will reduce the bureaucracy in the organization by making all management people aware of the actions they are taking that creates it.

This book was written with the idea that you could, if you choose, give your managers this book so that they can fully understand the nature of bureaucracy and what the organization will need to do to reduce or eliminate bureaucracy.

I suggest that your managers be involved participatively in deciding what to do about bureaucracy. Decide as a management team how far to go, and what level of effort and priority to give it.

Whatever level of attack you make on bureaucracy, I suggest managers learn about bureaucracy so they can understand what they do that fosters it, and what they can do to reduce it.

Teaching managers about bureaucracy

You can ask your training people to find or produce a course for your organization to use, based on the following set of principles and ideas.

You could use this book as advance reading, so everybody starts from the same place, and then have your trainers facilitate a program in which they learn, examine and practice the principles involved.

What follows is an abbreviated outline of the kind of instruction I would recommend.

Teach upper and middle managers the principles of sub-optimizing, so they won't mistakenly organize anything else sub-optimally.

I learned the concept of optimizing sub-functions from an executive at a large aircraft manufacturer. This lesson took place 33 years ago, and it has played an important part in my thinking ever since. I'll tell you what I remember of the example he used, and I hope those more familiar with the story will forgive me if I don't recount the story exactly. Anyway, it's the idea that counts.

■ *Evidently, this aircraft manufacturer had a number of plants all around the area, each making parts for airplanes that were then assembled into whole airplanes. Each plant had its own fleet of trucks that they used to pick up what they needed from other plants and from suppliers, and to deliver their sub-assemblies to the assembly plants.*

One day, somebody had the idea of centralizing the control of all the trucks into one motor pool. (This is the kind of "efficiency" argument that always seems to make good sense.) The idea was simple. At that time there were a large number of trucks, let's say 100. If, however, they were centralized, and dispatched by somebody who had the entire picture, the whole job could be done with fewer vehicles, let's say 60 trucks. Wow! The potential savings were tremendous. So, they centralized them. Now, instead of a truck going from plant A to plant B and coming back empty, the truck could pick up stuff from plant B and deliver it to plant D. Get the idea?

Well, what happened was that pretty quickly the plants noticed that when they needed an emergency pick up of parts to continue assembly, they didn't have a truck available. And, first once, then twice, then again and again, they found they had to stop work in their plants because they didn't have the parts they needed, and they didn't have the flexibility to dispatch "inefficient" emergency pickups to get their plants back to work. As my friend characterized it, "It almost brought us to our knees."

The story ended well, because the top executives realized that their goal was really to optimize building airplanes (their mission), rather than to optimize fleet dispatching (a process).

So, they gave the plants back their trucks, folded up the centralized motor pool and went back to being (happily and knowledgeably) "inefficient." Their plants hummed once again, and they had learned a valuable lesson about optimizing sub-functions.

In the last thirty-some years, I have been involved with hundreds of companies that have never learned about optimizing sub-functions, and I've seen the pain and misery that optimizing sub-functions causes.

Another example:

I will disguise this story enough to avoid embarrassing the organization that had the experience. It started the way that all sub-optimizing stories start. Somebody had an idea for more "efficiency."

■ *Let's say it was a large telephone company, and one day someone counted up the number of copiers in the 25-story building, and found that there were 118 copiers spread throughout the entire central office building. Eager to be "efficient" and desiring to be a hero, this person presented a proposal to management to replace the 118 different kinds and sizes of machines with 2 "power copiers" in a copying department. The proposal showed how the new copying department could be run* by two operators and a supervisor. It would use less space, and would save each secretary in the organization an estimated 14 minutes per day, which was the equivalent of 16 people saved, etc., etc.

So, without knowing it, the organization was off and running with a perfect example of optimizing a sub-function.

The company installed the copying department on the seventh floor, picked up all 118 copiers and began saving money.

The first day in operation, the copying department was besieged by secretaries (and other people) who wanted copies made, and there was a long line. Secretaries were waiting up to an hour to place their orders for copies. Within a day or two, everyone was aware that there were problems. So, they decided that all secretaries would "mail" their requests to copying, via inter-company mail, and the mail room would bring the finished copies back when they were done.

The first problem with that was that the mail room was only making two trips a day around the building, so turn-around on copies went to a minimum of two or even three days. So, they decided to add four people to the mail room, and double the number of trips around the building. This brought turnaround to two days "guaranteed."

Well, it turns out that two days was too long for certain "emergency" items, and for certain "high level" people, so a red tag was established to give certain items 24-hour turnaround. By now, however, there were two more people in the copying department. One was organizing inputs so the operators could keep on copying, and the other person took the outputs and addressed them to the people who needed them.

The next problem was that things started getting lost. People would send things to copying and never get anything back. And, other people were getting copies they hadn't ordered.

So, the copying department decided to add a series of controls to ensure nothing got lost, and a time stamp, because people were complaining that they weren't getting a two-day response.

This all required two more clerical people in the copying department to handle the complicated forms that were introduced so that nothing ever got lost.

By now, secretaries and their bosses were up in arms. They didn't trust the copying department with anything important, so for important items, they would stop by quick copy shops on the way home. And, a couple of departments pooled their petty cash to buy home-style, inexpensive copiers that they would use for urgent items.

Pretty soon, the accounting department became aware of the new "outside" copying costs, and individual departments were attempting to assign the outside copying costs to the copying department.

*The copying department then went to war (**with their own customers!**). They got a senior VP to issue a mandate that all personal copiers would be taken out immediately, citing some vague danger of liability or safety violations. In addition, the mandate stated that all "outside" copying would cease, and that the company would not pay for it.*

In an attempt to mollify the angry customers, the senior VP authorized a full second shift of operators and clerical people in the copying department, with a new guarantee of 24-hour turnaround time for everybody.

Well, I could go on with this story, because things actually got worse than this. By the end, every manager of any stature had a personal copier at home. There was a 24-hour quick copy shop down the street that would make copies, but issue invoices for "office supplies," that quickly became one of the top ten copy shops in the country for the franchisee.

And, worse than all of that, meetings couldn't be called on anything less than a one-week schedule to ensure that everyone got notified, and copies of the agenda were prepared, etc.

Now, you might think that all of this chaos would generate somebody who would say, "this isn't working, let's go back to the old way." But no. Sadly enough, this was a very bureaucratic organization (as if you hadn't guessed), and the powers that be were reluctant to admit they had made a mistake, so they just persisted.

What finally solved the problem was another bright young "efficiency" person who examined the situation and prepared another proposal to management. By now there were 17 people full time in two shifts in the copy department. The new proposal suggested that the 17 people department be disbanded, and replaced by 94 optimally situated copiers (of the same brand, size, and capability, because standardization was highly prized). The justification was the net savings of over $100,000 per year. So, in this case, the centralized copying department was disbanded, the 94 optimally-situated copiers were installed (all of the same size, brand and capability), and once again the organization was able to resume its normal work in a normal way.

I wish I could tell you that this organization had learned a lesson from this experience, and would be careful before they again optimized a sub-function. But I don't think they ever grasped the lesson that they had paid such a high price to learn.

In any case, I think it would be instructive to teach all of your managers the principles of optimizing sub-functions, so that your people learn to focus on *optimizing mission achievement*, and learn to tolerate a few "inefficiencies" in sub-functions along the way.

Here is another way of stating the message:

- It is **de-bureaucratizing** to take sub-optimized functional departments and disband them, re-deploying the people into the line units where they will be mission driven, not function driven. Here are some units to consider: purchasing, personnel, fleet, copying, MIS, training, strategic planning, budgeting, and research and development.

Teach your managers that it *fosters bureaucracy* to assign individuals or sub-groups a sub-optimal mission within the operating unit.

In a bureaucracy, departments or sub-units are formed and are allowed to, or even directed to, focus on a sub-optimal mission. "Your mission, in the copying department, is to handle all of the organization's copying needs at the lowest possible cost."

"Your mission, in the fleet department, is to optimize vehicle efficiency, and minimize the costs of trucking between all the plants and our suppliers."

Either of these sub-optimal missions could allow these support departments to bring the organization's mission to a standstill if the organization's mission interferes with the department's mission. It needs to be the other way around. Departments must support the organization's mission.

- It is **de-bureaucratizing** to assign individuals or sub-groups missions that are "nested" within the larger mission.

It isn't true that decentralizing is always better. Centralizing functions for "efficiency" isn't a great idea, but centralizing for "better support to mission achievers" may be acceptable. The key test is who decides whether they stay or go? If it's the internal customers, then centralizing can sometimes actually support mission achievement.

> *"The copying department's mission is to ensure that the organization's quality and customer satisfaction mission is achieved by ensuring that everyone who needs a copy gets one, as quickly and responsively as possible, with responsible regard for costs."*

This mission statement must be clearly understood to mean that if the copying department doesn't give its internal customers better service than they would get if they ran their own copying, then the unit will cease to function and copying will be decentralized. In addition, the performance of the copying department, and future budget allocations, will depend not on satisfying the manager the sub-unit reports to, but instead on feedback from the customers of the copying department.

> *"The fleet department's mission is to support our plants in achieving quality to standard and extraordinary customer satisfaction, and ensure that the plants—your customers— always have whatever vehicle they need to move parts and materials so that the plants always keep running."*

Again, this mission statement must be understood to mean that if the fleet department doesn't give the plants better and more responsive access to trucks than they had with their own fleet, the unit will be disbanded and trucking will be decentralized.

In addition, the future of the fleet department, and its budget allocations, will depend on customer satisfaction feedback from the plants it serves.

It fosters bureaucracy to assign decision-making authority based on levels in the organization rather than experience, training or proven judgment.

In bureaucracies, people are empowered to make decisions according to their level in the organization. The monetary limits of the decision may also be defined solely by the level in the organization. This results in two odd situations:

1. The odd situation of a newly named manager, coming from the outside or from a different chain of command, who is instantly empowered to make important decisions, who may have neither the experience, the training, nor proven judgment to make those decisions.

2. The odd situation of the seasoned career employee, who has the experience, the training and proven judgment to make critical decisions, having to report to and accept the decisions of the newly named manager, noted above.

It is *de-bureaucratizing* to delegate as many decisions as possible as close to the front line as possible, based on experience, training and proven judgment, rather than level in the organization.

The principles of empowerment (described in detail in Chapter 6) make it possible to empower people based on the importance of the decision, and the experience, training, and proven judgment of people.

The empowerment grid (Chapter 6) graphically shows how individuals can be empowered through a series of levels depending on the decision to be made, and the experience, training and proven judgment of the individual.

Empowerment in this manner ensures that people can make decisions that will be low risk, and at the same time allow for growth and responsibility to accrue to people based on their experience and skill, without depending on their "level" in the organization.

It is *bureaucratizing* to attempt to control people with rules, especially if those rules get in the way of achieving the mission.

A manager who issues "mandates" or "edicts" or "rules" is behaving in a manner that adds to the bureaucracy. Mandates, edicts and rules preclude the use of individual judgment and may, unintentionally, result in compromising the mission.

- It is **de-bureaucratizing** to participatively arrive at permissions, protection, and guidelines that people can use to govern their own actions. Managers then can replace *control* with *observing* and *coaching*. Managers can evaluate team or individual performance based on mission achievement rather than rule conformance.

When non-managers play a role in shaping the guidelines that will be used, and are empowered to put aside the guidelines when the mission is endangered, they are very likely to "buy in" to the guidelines and use them when they work to achieve the mission. Individuals can be held responsible for "pre-action" approval before abandoning guidelines in critical decision areas, or, for less critical decisions, can be scheduled for "post-action review," to allow for coaching and management guidance.

It is *bureaucratizing* to require pre-action sign-off before competent subordinates can act on matters within their area of expertise, because pre-action sign-offs disempower, create bottlenecks and destroy accountability.

Pre-action approvals can be useful in some cases. Sometimes the decision is just too critical to delegate. Sometimes the person isn't yet prepared by experience or training to make the decision. In these cases, requiring a pre-action approval can provide a good opportunity for developmental coaching.

If pre-action approvals are mandated for routine decisions or required of people with proven experience, training and judgment, then pre-action approvals are bureaucratizing, disempowering and pose a grave risk to the improvement of quality or customer satisfaction.

- It is **de-bureaucratizing** to replace pre-action review with post-action review in those situations where external controls are needed (and where the individuals have the appropriate skills, training or experience to make the necessary decisions.) Post-action review allows people to act as needed to achieve the quality or customer satisfaction mission, and then, in situations that require strict controls, be accountable to explain the actions they took.

It *fosters bureaucracy* to behave as though employees can't be trusted to work without being pushed, and can't be trusted to make good judgments on issues relating to their jobs.

Douglas McGregor, in his book *The Human Side of Enterprise,* first characterized "Theory X and Theory Y Managers." McGregor was also describing the difference between assumptions inherent in the bureaucratic model of organization and the modern, "mission-driven" model this book recommends.

McGregor characterized the Theory X manager as one who believes (or at least acts as though he/she believes) that employees have to be pushed to get them to work.

McGregor characterized the Theory Y manager as one who believes that employees enjoy working, and will work hard without being driven.

Virtually every manager who has had any formal management training has been exposed to the Theory X/Y model. As I have learned more about the debilitating effects of using the bureaucratic model of organizing, I have concluded that Theory X management styles are part and parcel of the bureaucratic model.

I can add two observations to reinforce what McGregor noticed in his Theory X/Y descriptions:

1. Both Theory X and Theory Y managers prove themselves right in their assumptions, because each theory tends to be self-fulfilling. That is, if you treat people as though they won't work unless pushed, they generally won't. And, if you treat people as though they can be trusted to work without being pushed, they generally will.

2. Changing from a Theory X to Theory Y type management style often is not successful in a bureaucratic organization. This is an example of trying to eliminate bureaucracy by fighting one of its symptoms. You may change that symptom, but you do nothing to affect the root cause. I think this explains why Theory Y managers often experience frustration, and sometimes fail to thrive in a Theory X-based bureaucratic environment.

When the organization changes from the bureaucratic model of organizing to a mission-driven model, the underlying assumption on which the entire model is based shifts from Theory X assumptions to Theory Y assumptions. This underlying paradigm shift makes it not only comfortable, but relatively easy to shift from Theory X to Theory Y-type management styles. To summarize for clarity:

- It is **de-bureaucratizing** to behave as though lower-level employees *can* be trusted to work without being pushed, and to begin with the assumption that *they have good judgment* and will use it if given the encouragement and authority to do so. If individuals fail to live up to expectations, they can be dealt with on an individual basis.

It is *bureaucratizing* to carve out turf, defend that turf and require others to inform you or get your input prior to making any decisions which might be interpreted as falling within your "turf." (This inhibits mission achievement and creates dependence rather than independence.)

Functional experts, with specialized knowledge, are encouraged by the bureaucratic model to consider their expertise as the source of their power and to jealously guard their authority as the expert. Part of this difficulty stems from organizing people into units based on what work they do, rather than what outcomes you want them to achieve. This creates departmental walls that have to be crossed to get work done. Another part of this difficulty comes from allowing these functional units to have missions that aren't "nested" within the organization's mission, so you have the odd result of work units that actually interfere with achieving the organization's mission, as they jealously guard their "turf."

- It is **de-bureaucratizing** to teach, grow and empower others to make choices or decisions in areas in which you have expertise. Ideally, you use your knowledge and expertise to support mission achievement, and to create independence rather than dependence. Hopefully, the functional expertise is not all collected together in one department, but disseminated throughout the organization within multi-disciplinary teams, with perhaps a small staff support team of coaches.

It is *bureaucratizing* to require that individuals communicate through the "chain of command" instead of directly with the people they need to deal with.

If Sally in department A needs to talk to Brenda in department B, some organizations require that she talk first to her boss, who then talks to Brenda's boss, then Brenda's boss talks to Brenda. This is called "following the chain of command." Supposedly, it keeps everyone that needs to know informed. What it really does is stifle communication, hinder problem solving and put an obstacle in the path of Sally achieving her quality or customer satisfaction mission.

- It is **de-bureaucratizing** to encourage people to deal directly with the people they need to deal with to achieve the quality or customer satisfaction mission. Modern communication technology and new communication disciplines can ensure that everyone who needs to be informed stays informed.

When you delegate the authority to talk to whoever is needed to achieve the mission, it is important to also delegate the responsibility for ensuring that everyone who needs to be informed is informed. Modern technology like electronic mail and telephone messaging systems can facilitate complete information exchange. In the mission-driven model of organizing, however, bosses don't need to be kept informed of routine transactions just because they are bosses. The idea that the boss of a unit must know everything that happens in that unit is a vestige of the bureaucratic model.

It *fosters bureaucracy* to organize so as to require front-line people to cross departmental walls in order to access the support they need to achieve their mission. The more walls that must be crossed, the more opportunities there are for system snafus, delays and customer frustration.

Multi-disciplinary teams and cross-functional task forces are a way of life in the search for service quality and customer satisfaction.

- It is **de-bureaucratizing** to organize so that every human and material resource needed to satisfy the mission is available to front-line people from within the work unit, thus eliminating "turf boundaries" that have to be crossed.

It *fosters bureaucracy* to allow rules, guidelines, procedures, policies or practices to stand unexamined in the face of employee or customer dissatisfaction or product quality failure. In this context, rules are made dominant to the mission.

- It is **de-bureaucratizing** to consider that rules, guidelines, policies, practices or procedures are tools designed to help achieve customer and employee satisfaction or product quality. From that standpoint, when faced with poor product quality, or an employee or customer that is dissatisfied, it is de-bureaucratizing to assume that the person is "right" and the rule, policy, etc., needs to be examined.

It is *bureaucratizing* to ration information. Information, when rationed, becomes a tool to support power or dependence, and rationing it creates feelings of being excluded or "shut out" of the team or mission by those who don't have access.

- It is **de-bureaucratizing** to make information available freely as needed or as desired. Information empowers, sponsors innovation and creativity, and creates the experience of being "included" as part of the larger team or mission. It isn't necessarily the information itself. Having free *access* to it, even if people don't take advantage of the access, is almost equal to actually getting it.

It is *bureaucratizing* for a work unit to issue rules that are annoying or burdensome to those served by the work unit.

- It is **de-bureaucratizing** for a work unit to issue guidelines (rather than rules) that make things better, easier and simpler for the *people served by the work unit.* Work units will have to accept less consistency and allow more flexibility. This is the price a work unit pays to serve its internal customers in an extraordinary fashion.

Conclusion

When the managers in your organization understand and can explain the basic concepts in this section, you can feel confident that they have the knowledge they need to support your organization's transition from a bureaucratic model to a mission-driven organization.

Whether your managers actually begin to operate in the new mode will depend on how much support there is in the environment for them to change.

If you, as senior management, learn and use the ideas in this section, then through your modeling and leadership, you will increase the odds that managers throughout the organization will adopt the de-bureaucratizing behaviors.

I recommend that you teach everyone in the organization these concepts. Then, if someone slips up and forgets these principles, others will be able to prompt them. This sort of "cross coaching" would be useful in changing a bureaucratic culture.

If you really want to nail down the change, you will install employee feedback systems that provide feedback to each manager from those who work for the manager, as well as the manager's peers. When these new forms of feedback are combined with the traditional feedback from the manager's boss, they form a complete picture. Then, everyone who continues to operate in the bureaucratic mold to the detriment of mission achievement, can get the feedback they need to help them change to de-bureaucratizing strategies.

Summary

• This chapter outlines a training program that might be considered the minimum needed to equip managers with the skills and attitudes and strategies they will need to manage in the non-bureaucratic manner required by customer-focused or customer-driven goal states.

   a. Avoid sub-optimization (optimizing sub functions instead of mission-oriented functions).

   b. "Nest" departmental missions so they support rather than confound the organization's overall mission.

   c. Empower people to make decisions based on experience, training and proven judgment, rather than organizational level.

   d. Delegate decision authority as close to the front line as possible.

   e. Manage by empowering, coaching and removing obstacles, rather than by criticizing and disciplining.

   f. Trust employees and assume that they will work because they are internally motivated—unless or until they demonstrate that they cannot be trusted or require external motivation—and to treat each employee as an individual case.

   g. Teach, grow and empower others with your expertise, rather than hoarding it and using it to become irreplaceable.

   h. Encourage people to work directly with those they need to deal with, rather than requiring conformance to a "chain of command."

   i. Group people together into multi-functional or multi-disciplinary teams to eliminate walls that must be crossed to achieve the unit's mission.

   j. Subordinate policies, practices and procedures to mission achievement.

   k. Organize in ways that make things easier for customers of the unit, rather than to make things easy for the unit.

Chapter Sixteen

To reduce or eliminate the negative effects of bureaucracy, you'll need the help and support of the employees who are not in management

Preview

This chapter is about and for your non-managerial people. This contains an outline of the communications or training that you may want to give them so they fully understand the efforts you want to make toward de-bureaucratization or the continuous improvement of quality, service, or both.

Once your front-line people understand and believe that you want to de-bureaucratize, or become mission driven, you will discover that they will be your strongest supporters. Reactions will range from, "I can't believe they finally figured it out," to "We've been telling them this for years, but they just wouldn't listen."

If your people are unionized, and the union management is still in the dark ages, then you will likely get some resistance from the union management. But, trust your people. Once they understand that you are serious, that you really want to "turn the pyramid upside down" to achieve quality to standard or service quality that produces customer satisfaction, they'll get the message to the union. What you are doing is *right*. You'll know that, and your people will know that. Trust that basic idea, and work with your people to find a way to come together, as one enormous team, to move away from bureaucracy and toward a mission driven by quality and customer satisfaction.

Feel free to turn the ideas that follow over to your people if you want to invent your own training solution. Or, if you want to get a head start before you can roll out formal training, you might want to circulate copies of this book so that your non-management people will understand what you and your management team are undertaking.

If there is a large gulf of misunderstanding and mistrust between your management and your people, then you might well let somebody who is an outsider deliver the message. By circulating this book among your people, you are letting me tell them what I think they need to know about the shift to a quality or customer satisfaction mission.

Whether you let me tell them, through copies of this book, or get someone else to tell them, here are the things I think they need to eventually understand.

A message for all employees:

This isn't just another "program."

It isn't aimed at getting more out of labor's hide for fewer bucks. It isn't just another battle in the labor/management war. If you and your fellow employees join in the commitment to a customer or quality focus, with the goal of eliminating bureaucracy, the war is over!

The successful Japanese companies are not at war with themselves. They operate as one team, in harmony, with a quality focus and a long-term view. For your organization to thrive, all sides must put away their self-centered views and disarm. What's needed is one team, with one vision.

The labor/management fight is over. The line/staff fight is over. The headquarters/field fight is over. People, whether labor, manager, professional, staff, or administration, who continue to act as though they are at war with some other part of the organization will be standing in the way of your organization achieving its mission.

Sure, you'll need some time to adjust. You'll need time to give up obsolete ways of thinking, and to adopt the new model. But, if you are steeped in the old ways of internal strife and warfare, you must change or get out. Otherwise, you'll hurt your organization, and that's not what they're paying you to do, or why you joined the organization in the first place.

When management asks front-line people to participate in something as all-encompassing as a new vision, or getting rid of bureaucracy, the first and most natural response is often fear.

To conquer the fear, learn and understand the process, and your role in it.

It's a new game, and from now on, it's customer satisfaction, or quality, or both, that count. Management has wised up to the realization that profit is a by-product of quality products or customer satisfaction. You don't achieve extraordinary quality or service by managing *profits*. You achieve extraordinary quality or service by managing *quality or service*.

If you think this is just this year's program, you may well be mistaken. The intention is for a lifetime change. The objective is a permanent organization-wide shift in the vision, the goal and the culture.

- Stop watching the boss—watch the customer, or the quality of your outputs, or both.

- Stop focusing on "your turf" or "your rights"—it's not an internal war any more. Focus on what *you* are contributing to satisfying the customer.

- If you currently have a union, you'll soon have another union —a union of all the people in your organization coming together as one team. If the present union management catches on to this wave and supports you in making the transition, there will still be an important role for the union to play. If they get in the way of this change, you may have to leave them behind, or vote in a new union that sees the importance of the new mission.

- If you're not serving the customer, you're probably serving someone who is. If your job is to serve someone within the organization, then your new challenge is to give your *internal* customers the same extraordinary service or quality that your organization wants to give to *external* customers.

- Increasingly our economy is based on service. In a service world, we owe each other good service. Here's what I call the social compact: In a service economy, we take turns serving each other. When it's our turn to serve, we give the customer the deference, the respect and the dignity that customers deserve. When it's our turn to be served, we can then expect, and even insist on, the deference, the respect and the dignity that we deserve.

- Whoever you're serving, give them the things they want from a service provider. Customers want friendly and caring service, they want you to be flexible, they want you to help them resolve problems when they're stuck, and they want you to recover when you make a mistake or the organization goofs.

Whether you have internal customers for the outputs of your work, or you serve external customers, here is what your customers want.

First, they want you to provide the basic service that is your job to provide and they expect that service to be at a level of quality up to agreed-upon standards. But, unfortunately, they won't give you much credit for just providing your expected, basic, quality service.

To dazzle your customers, you will need to do all of the next four things as well.

- They want you to be friendly and caring. When you are getting service, you want the service provider to care about satisfying you, and to be friendly and easy to do business with. Well, so do your customers (internal or external).

- If they aren't perfectly satisfied with the service you offer them, and they want something different, they want you to be flexible.

  Stretch, and jiggle the system, for the customer. Pay attention to the outcome, not the process.

- If they are stuck and can't figure out the system or don't know what to do next, they want you to help them problem solve, whether it's a business problem or not. It's no good thinking that "it's not my job," because in the service world, whether it's an internal or external customer, it *is* your job.

- Finally, they want you to recover when your unit or the organization goofs.

  - Admit it when there has been a mistake, and apologize on behalf of yourself, the work unit, or the organization.

  - Make it right, if you can.

  - Go the extra step; provide something, at least some form of symbolic atonement.

  - Follow up to be sure the customer is satisfied and the recovery is complete.

The organization and its people can't and won't change overnight.

We're all human. If you and your associates take this new commitment very seriously and don't make any big missteps during the transition, it'll still take years before you're where you want to be. I've been observing some really good people in some really good companies making this transition, and it never goes as fast as it seems it should, or as fast as you want it to. However, the act of starting begins a momentum that grows and grows until the transformation has an energy of its own that pulls you along.

Remember, it isn't just management who has to change; bureaucracy contaminates everyone in the organization.

In bureaucracy, you find yourself waiting for someone to tell you what to do—when you need to be taking your own initiatives. You'll find yourself afraid to act for fear of being wrong when you need to act. In the "new" organization, you need to have the courage of your convictions. You'll find that bureaucracy has taken a lot away, and you'll need to take conscious steps if you want to really pull your weight toward achieving the mission.

- Part of your job will be to get comfortable with responsibility and to take risks (if you need to) to achieve the mission.

- Part of your job will be to get comfortable with the idea of pro-activity and initiative. In a bureaucracy, people didn't ask you to take initiatives and even made life difficult for you if you did. In a mission-driven organization, you'll need to step up to the situation if quality or customer satisfaction are threatened.

- I think it's also part of your job to get in, get out, or keep quiet. I put this part in so you can point it out to any of your fellow employees who want to keep up the old, internal cold-war.

Cynics don't help.
Blamers don't help.
Complainers and
whiners don't
help. Help if
you can. Get
out if you
can't help.
And, if you
can't help,
or get out—
keep quiet.

- Be a cheer-
leader and a coach if you want to really help.

You'll be asked for feedback; give it straight, make it helpful.

Even if you have a long history of being asked and never hearing anything back, open up and give feedback when it's requested. Sometime during the transition you'll actually start getting feedback back after you send it up the line.

- At some point, people are going to ask you, "How good is your boss at supporting you in your role?" This isn't an opportunity to get back for all those years of suffering. This is a time to take your responsibilities seriously, and give straight and honest feedback.

- They're going to ask you to give feedback to others on your team (your peers) so that they can learn to be good team players. The idea is to change the feedback system so that feedback about performance and contribution doesn't all just come from the top down. Eventually, you'll be getting feedback from those you serve, from your peers, and from your manager. The feedback will be less painful because it won't be coming from the perspective of monitoring, controlling, and disciplining that marked the bureaucratic system. Instead, the feedback you'll be getting will be more from the perspective of coaching, so you can become a more valuable member of the team.

- If you serve internal or external customers, you'll be asked what your customers say they want from you or your work unit. It's now well understood that people who serve customers are a good proxy for the customers themselves. So, you'll be asked for your ideas on what the organization can do to support you in satisfying your customers.

- You'll be asked, "What policies, practices and procedures stand in the way of you achieving quality to standard, or serving your customers well?" Keep alert for situations where you aren't able to satisfy your customers because of an interfering policy, practice or procedure. When you're asked, tell them what is getting in your customers' way.

- Departments that serve you will be asking you, "How well are you being served by the people, policies, practices and procedures of the work units that serve you?" Don't hurt, but don't hold back. Be straight, say what you think and feel, so people can learn what it will take to give you extraordinary service. Don't make them guess.

- You'll be asked, "What suggestions can you make that will improve the products or services that you are providing your customers?" Perhaps for the first time the organization will really be receptive to suggestions and ideas. The bureaucratic defensiveness and turf protection that squelched so many good ideas in the past will gradually disappear.

Summary

• This chapter outlines the changes that non-management people will need to learn as they assume the larger role they will undertake in the success of a non-bureaucratic organization.

a. They'll need to understand this isn't just another "program of the year." This is a permanent change in the structure, goals and mission of the organization.

b. They'll need to understand that fear, anxiety and mistrust are natural. They are rooted in the traditional alienation between management and "labor" that is produced by the bureaucratic organizing model.

c. They'll need to learn that the game has changed. The old rules don't work any more. There are new rules to learn.

d. They'll need to learn that the customer or quality is king in the new way of working.

e. They'll need to learn that they have a customer for their work, even if it isn't the ultimate customer the organization serves. They'll need to learn to give their customers quality work and excellent service.

f. They'll need to learn patience, and to learn that change comes hard and doesn't happen over night. They'll learn that neither they nor their managers will convert their actions or attitudes from the bureaucratic model to the new model overnight.

g. They'll need to learn to give feedback and to take feedback from customers and from their peers, subordinates, teammates, and bosses.

h. They'll need to learn to think in new ways about their union, if they have one. They'll need to learn to know when the union is supporting organizational success through promoting worker harmony, or when the union is promoting organizational failure by exploiting worker alienation.

Chapter Seventeen

You'll need to change your culture by changing some beliefs, taboos and traditions that may be basic to your culture currently

Preview

You can use this chapter to stimulate discussion about how the culture needs to change as you move away from the bureaucratic form. Beliefs and taboos are basic to your culture. As you change the beliefs and taboos, your culture will change in response. This chapter contains the beliefs inherent to the bureaucratic form that will need to be re-examined and changed to fit your new model.

Here is a list of beliefs that will need to be gradually changed as your culture adapts to the new model.

It is bureaucratic to think that all functions of planning and control have to be done by management.

To be customer focused or achieve total quality, much of the planning, controlling, reacting, responding and flexing must be done by front-line people—by people who don't manage others, but manage the achievement of quality, or who manage the satisfaction of customers.

It is bureaucratic to think that managers and managing are more important than the people who achieve the quality or satisfy individual customers. It is bureaucratic to think that the higher you are on the organization chart, the more important you are.

Those who strive to become customer focused or to achieve total quality soon discover that the truly "important" people are the ones who are part of achieving the total quality or who satisfy the customers. Regardless of what management wants, says or does, if the front-line people aren't on the team, the mission doesn't get achieved. Team members understand that it hurts teamwork to rank team members in terms of importance. Every job and every role is important. Eventually, relative status and importance becomes much less of an issue.

It seems to be a basic precept of bureaucracy that ambiguity is intolerable and must be resolved. Things must be black or white. There is no room for gray.

To achieve total quality or to consistently dazzle customers, your organization and your people must have some tolerance for ambiguity. You have to deal in the real world, facing real problems and real people. In the real world, there is a lot of gray. If you attempt to make things black or white, you miss too much. Rules can be unambiguous, while guidelines are ambiguous, e.g., "If the guidelines don't work to achieve the mission, then forget the guidelines and do what it takes achieve the mission." That's pretty gray.

The most widely held, and perhaps the most damaging, belief underlying bureaucracy is the belief that consistency, itself, has value.

Consistency is very important in piece parts that make up a product. And, in the absence of good reason for changing, consistency has value in relationships. But, consistency in choices or decisions can sometimes be a barrier to good quality, or to satisfying customers.

Objective observers will notice that much of the damage to quality or to customer satisfaction comes from the importance that bureaucracies attach to the idea of consistency, without regard for the outcomes produced by an excessive concern for consistency.

For those striving for quality or customer satisfaction, it is valuable to believe that consistency is nice and comfortable as long as it achieves the desired quality or results in satisfied customers. But, the moment that it gets in the way of quality or customer satisfaction, forget consistency and substitute flexibility.

A sister to the idea of consistency is the idea that equal treatment for everybody is fair for all. All you can say about equal treatment for all is that it will result in unequal satisfaction for all. Bureaucracies value the process of equal treatment, but ignore the outcome of unequal satisfaction.

If you strive for an objective outcome, like quality in your product, or customer satisfaction from your service, then examine the idea that equal treatment for all is good. I suggest to you that *equal satisfaction* for all customers is a better strategy than *equal treatment* for all customers.

How do you want to be measured—by the treatment you give or by the outcome you achieve? Customers are only interested in getting satisfied. If equal treatment doesn't satisfy them, then they expect you to treat them unequally. If you are legally or morally wedded to the conclusion that unequal treatment is unjust, then pay attention to the idea of choices. Giving the customer lots of choices makes it possible to provide as many different treatments as customers tell you they need in order to be satisfied.

■ *One example is the Florida Department of Motor Vehicles, the people who provide drivers' licenses. Until recently, they treated everybody the same. To get a license, you went to the office and stood in line. They didn't give appointments. By treating everybody the same, they made some people really dissatisfied.*

Then, they began offering appointments. If time is important to the customer, the customer can call up for an appointment. If time isn't that important, or you need something today, you can come anytime and wait in line. By offering a choice, they increased the number of citizens who are satisfied with their service.

Another false belief that is common in bureaucracies is the idea of the "slippery slope": "If I do it for one, I have to do it for everybody."

This is an argument that pops up almost automatically in bureaucratic thinking, and is another sister to the belief in consistency and equal treatment for all. This idea is so pervasive because there are some situations in which it is true. The error is in over-generalizing the idea and applying it where it is patently false and sometimes even foolish.

Organizations that value total quality or customer focus want their people to make decisions and choices based on the mission outcome and not on the process. So, the process becomes much more flexible, as long as it is aimed at achieving the desired outcome. If you have to wrap the product in green to satisfy this customer, you wrap it in green. If you have to deliver the paper to the third floor for this customer, you deliver it to the third floor. You trust that people are reasonable and understanding, and you realize that "flexing" the process to satisfy one customer doesn't mean that you will have to make that same accommodation to all customers.

Because of the hierarchy and control from the top that characterize bureaucracies, choices are often thought to be confusing to customers and employees.

The reality is that choices are confusing *to those making up the rules,* and to keep their job simple, they tend to minimize the number of choices given to customers and employees. It might even be generalized to say, "The more bureaucratic the organization, the fewer choices offered to customers and employees."

Organizations that empower their employees to make decisions aimed at satisfying customers find that the employees will create lots and lots of choices for customers. That is because customers really like to be satisfied, and the more choices there are, the more likely it is the customer will find one that satisfies.

It is bureaucratic to believe that "efficiency" is more important than achieving the mission.

It is de-bureaucratizing to put mission achievement ahead of "efficiency." This is the essence of being mission-driven rather than being in-focused.

It is bureaucratic to act as though the process is more important than outcomes.

It is de-bureaucratizing to focus on the outcomes and adjust processes as needed to ensure that the outcome is in harmony with the mission.

It is bureaucratic to manage with a "problem-solving" approach.

In the problem-solving approach, someone—usually a manager—looks at a problem, "fixes" that problem, then moves on to the next one, without addressing the root cause and with no encouragement to address the root cause.

It is de-bureaucratizing to empower teams of people to be responsible for dealing with barriers to achieving the mission.

When quality or customer satisfaction is everyone's goal, then problems don't have to be solved by managers alone. Empowered people, aspiring to continuous improvement, can be trained to not only solve the immediate problem, but also to find the root causes and fix them.

Summary

- This chapter outlines some of the basic beliefs that are part and parcel of the bureaucratic organizing model—beliefs that will have to be re-examined if individuals are to put aside bureaucracy and adapt to a new organizing model.

  a. Planning and control can be done by teams as well or better than by individual managers.

  b. Managers are not any more or less important than non-managers. Importance has to do with contribution to the mission rather than organizational level.

  c. Ambiguity *is* tolerable, and in many cases even desirable.

  d. Consistency can, and even should, be put aside anytime it interferes with mission achievement.

  e. Equal treatment for all (customers or employees) results in unequal satisfaction. A better goal is equal satisfaction —at a very high level. To achieve equal satisfaction requires differences in treatment for customers and employees.

  f. In most cases, there is no "slippery slope." It is seldom true that "if I do it for one, I have to do it for all."

  g. It is a good thing to offer many choices to customers and to employees. It is a vast variety of choices that makes it possible to treat people unequally and to make possible high levels of satisfaction.

  h. Efficiency is not more important than the mission. Achieving the mission is far more important than being efficient.

  i. Process is not more important than the outcome. Mission achievement cannot be subordinated to the importance of following any given process.

  j. Problem-solving is not solely a management skill. Teams of non-managers can be trained to identify and prioritize problems, and to solve them using the most sophisticated tools available.

Chapter Eighteen

How will you know when you have realized your vision?

Preview

This chapter offers an outline of ways by which one might form a "vision" of what the organization will be like in the future. To move away from bureaucracy, it is useful to have a "vision" of the new, more desirable, goal state. If your organization were to adopt a "customer-sensitive," "customer-focused" or "customer-driven" goal state, this chapter tells you how to know what your organization might be like when you are nearing your goal.

The transition to a "customer-focused" or "customer-driven" organization will really never be done. Just as you haven't become as totally bureaucratized as it is possible to become, you will never achieve being totally "customer focused" or "customer driven."

Tom Peters, author of *Thriving on Chaos*, characterized this as "the race that never ends."

On the other hand, you will inevitably shift from one mind-set to another. Your organization will move, grudgingly at first, then slowly, then faster, then faster yet, and at some point you can stop pushing and the momentum of the transformation will carry everyone along with it.

What follows are some tests you can use to determine whether you have shifted from the existing bureaucratic way of thinking to the new "mission-driven" model.

You'll know by the feedback you get from your customers and from your fellow employees.

Your customer will give you feedback in two different ways, solicited and unsolicited.

Unsolicited customer feedback

Currently, if your organization is fairly bureaucratic, you may get more negative unsolicited feedback than positive. As you transition to a "customer-focused" organization, the unsolicited feedback will shift from complaints and criticisms to letters of thanks and appreciation.

It often happens that negative letters are aimed toward the top of the organization. People write to the president, managing director, secretary, or CEO. They have a complaint and they want it heard.

When you have the right mission—and your organization is achieving its mission of *more* than satisfying your customers—then the organization will get a lot more unsolicited feedback of a very positive kind.

If you are a product-oriented organization and the quality of your product is noticeable to the customers, then you'll generally get positive letters, and because there is little personal contact they may be directed toward the top of the organization.

If you are a service-oriented organization, and your customer service is dazzling, then many of the positive letters will be directed toward people on the front lines. If you want the power of that positive feedback to nourish the entire organization you'll want to have an organized way to collect those praise and appreciation letters and publish them internally so everyone can share in the glow of customer satisfaction and the recipient can get the special recognition he or she deserves.

Even after you've made the transition you'll still get critical letters and suggestions, but the tone will be entirely different. The tone of the letters will reflect the customer's perception that your organization is really extraordinary. For example:

"I know how important customer service is to you, so I was shocked when..."

"I'm so used to the extraordinary quality of your products, I was surprised to find..."

"Your products are truly the highest quality and value, and your customer service is outstanding. That's why I'm wondering why you don't..."

Solicited customer feedback

You couldn't have achieved the transition to a "mission-driven" organization without *soliciting* feedback from your customers. So, I feel confident that you will have a history of feedback. If you take my recommendations, you will have a continuous flow of feedback over the duration of the transition. You'll be tracking service quality through focus panels, telephone "quality of service" calls and other types of surveys.

You will have changed your organization's view about negative feedback from customers. You will now eagerly search for negatives, and use them as "diagnostics" to help you improve further. You will have long since gotten over the bureaucratic tendency to be defensive about negative feedback, and you will have stopped "shooting the messenger."

As you transition toward a "customer-driven" organization, you will drive the scores on your feedback systems upward gradually, until the customer feedback shows that you are consistently exceeding customer expectations. Your scores will indicate that your typical customer is more than "satisfied." Your typical customer may be characterized as "pleased," "happy," "delighted," "dazzled" or even "loyal." You will find that your least-satisfied customers are still fairly "satisfied."

By the time you've "arrived," you will have learned that customer expectations are constantly changing, and they will rise as your product quality or service quality grows, so you are chasing a moving target. That's OK, because when you have achieved your mission, your customer feedback will show that your product or service quality meets or exceeds even the customer's increased expectations.

Employee feedback

Your employee feedback will also tell you when you have really transitioned from in-focused and bureaucratic to "customer focused" and "customer driven."

By tracking employee attitudes and perceptions regularly, you will have a moving record of your progress.

Don't expect that employees will stop having gripes and complaints. They will, even in the finest organization in the world, still find valid reasons for complaint.

Don't expect that very many employees will "appreciate" all that the organization is doing for them, or how much better it is now than it used to be.

Don't expect your employees to "praise" you or management for the great job you did in transforming the organization. Instead you'll hear things like, "Why didn't they do it sooner" and "They finally listened to us."

What you can look for in employee feedback is a shift in the focus and the importance of the complaints or suggestions.

In bureaucratic organizations, the focus of complaints is on the individual who has the complaint, or that person's peer group.

"I feel I've been unfairly treated..."

"It isn't fair that after all this time of being overworked, I am now being asked to..."

"The full burden of this downsizing is falling on me and my fellow administrative people..."

"The secretaries in this organization are not being fairly..."

In "mission-driven" organizations, the *focus* of complaints and suggestions tends to shift from the individual to the product, the service, the procedure, the practice, etc., generally related to the mission.

"I can't ever get to zero defects if I have to use this obsolete piece of equipment. We need a new..."

"I've had three customers in the last week go away frustrated because the information they want doesn't show up on the computer screen. We have to change the computer system as soon as possible."

As you become more customer driven, the importance of the issues being complained about increases as well.

Instead of: "I have to walk more than 75 feet to get to the rest room from my desk..."

you'll get: "I resent being measured on the number of calls I take each day from customers. Even if my manager doesn't use that data on my evaluation, I feel pressured to hurry, instead of taking the time needed to be certain the customer is satisfied."

You'll know by what your people are doing.

One way to track your progress is to ask all of your fellow executives and managers to keep a one- or two-week log of how they spent their time. Then, each year, repeat the experiment. Over time, you'll be able to measure the organization's progress in the transition by how people spend their time.

In a full-fledged bureaucracy the senior executives and upper-middle managers are likely to spend the bulk of their time in meetings. Those meetings are most likely focused on issues that are in-focused (things that are in the best interests of the organization, or a department within the organization).

When you have "arrived," your fellow executives will spend more time on strategic issues and allocating resources based on customer and employee feedback aimed at achieving the mission.

There will be fewer meetings. Your executives will spend more time "walking the talk," listening and learning. The action will be on the front lines and with the customers, and you can expect to find your executives where the action is. Your executives will be much closer to the customers and be far more accurate when they talk about "what customers want." Your fellow executives will be much closer to the people who are really responsible for achieving the mission—the people in the teams on the front lines.

When the executives are in meetings, the meetings will be far more often focused on issues related to the mission. Your executives will tend to be talking about and working on issues related to improving quality or dazzling customers. The internal issues being dealt with will also relate to the mission. They'll be talking about how to recognize service quality "heroes." They'll be dealing with how to create better internal service, so all employees will be getting extraordinary service from internal service providers. Every decision will be examined for its impact on customer satisfaction.

Your middle managers and supervisors will have different roles.

Your middle managers and front-line managers will have entirely different roles as your organization becomes more customer driven. Your managers will no longer concentrate on "control" or manage through power, intimidation and discipline. Your managers will manage by "modeling," "removing obstacles" and "coaching."

The managers will *model* your organizations mission. They will align with the mission and be incredibly focused on creating the quality or service that it takes to delight or dazzle your customers.

The managers in your organization will spend their time supporting the success of the teams that are actually achieving your mission. Their job will be to "remove obstacles" for the teams, and "run interference" inside the organization, as needed, to make it possible for the teams to achieve the mission.

When managers observe performance that is less than desired, they will operate as "coaches," rather than resorting to the discipline that was the strategy of choice when the organization was a bureaucracy. (Discipline may have value when "management" is on one team and "the workers" are on another. Indeed, the alienation in a bureaucracy can become so great that discipline is the only strategy that has any effect.)

Coaches, however, are on the same team as the players. Their goal is the same as the players. They want the players to succeed, and as coaches, their job is to teach when skills are needed, remind when concentration wavers, inspire when the will falters and cheer when a job is well done.

It has been often noted that getting middle managers "on board" is the hardest task of organizational transformation. I think that may be because the manager's role changes more completely than the role of the executives or the front-line people. For this reason, a careful monitoring of the changes in the middle managers' roles may be a very good indicator of how well the transition is going.

Your staff people will be almost entirely at the service of the mission achievers on the front lines.

Within a bureaucracy, staff people focus the bulk of their time and attention on serving the executive ranks. The mission of the staff units becomes the same as the mission of the executives. Typically, that is an in-focused mission, such as reducing costs, minimizing inventory, etc.

You'll know when your organization becomes "customer focused" or "customer driven" because the staff units will take strategic and financial direction from executives, and operating direction from the front lines.

For example, the purchasing department (if it hasn't been broken up and integrated into the multi-functional teams) might still set inventory investment limits based on executive direction, but it will truly become a support function for the front-line teams. Purchasing will be committed to helping the front-line teams achieve their service quality goals, and their success will depend on feedback from the front-line teams.

The second thing to look for is a major reduction in the number of people within staff departments. There may be some senior staff coordinators, but most of the people will be spread throughout the organization where they are really needed (for example, purchasing, training, etc.).

Those staff departments that formerly provided extensive support to in-focused missions, but didn't do anything to support the front lines, may have virtually disappeared. For example, I would expect to see functions like "strategic planning" and "budgeting" cut way back or eliminated totally. Customer-driven organizations do their planning and budgeting on a "bottom-up" basis, rather than "top down" as is done in the bureaucracy.

Within the operating units, or even at the team level, you might find people who, as part of their role, do the budgeting for their units. Once the organization really has a customer-focused mission, strategic planning, where necessary, will most likely be done by senior executives in response to inputs from task forces and front-line teams, using feedback from customers.

Your front-line people, organized as natural work units, cross-functional teams, or multi-disciplinary teams, will be responsible for creating the desired product quality or dazzling customer service that is their mission.

In customer-driven organizations, your front-line people won't be standing around waiting for instructions from above. They'll know what's needed, and they'll be "empowered" to do what's needed. Front-line people won't need to be "motivated" by prods from supervisors, higher pay, or more overtime. They'll be motivated by "the job itself," now that they understand how their work supports the mission. They'll be motivated by the "growth" that they've attained as they've learned the skills needed to do their job at the highest level of skill, and the additional developmental skills attendant with self-management.

Your people will be motivated by the "responsibility" that has become theirs as the teams have become responsible for the mission—rather than management.

Your people will be motivated by the "achievement" that comes from finishing a job high in quality, or from dazzling customers.

Your people will be motivated by the "recognition" that comes from being a service quality "hero" or from being part of a winning team.

Your people will be having fun on the job and won't be experiencing the stress that comes from being alienated from management, fearful of being disciplined and de-humanized by being treated like a unit of production.

An ironic note: Back in the 1950s and 1960s, management teams were studying the findings of Dr. Frederick Herzberg on motivation of employees. They were looking for ways to "enrich" jobs to give workers more motivation by adding the "motivators" to jobs such as: growth, recognition, responsibility, achievement and work that itself was interesting, stimulating or challenging.

Looking back, we can now see that the scarcity of success stories was caused by the underlying bureaucracy, rather than any failure in the Herzberg research or resultant theory. When you begin to partially or wholly put aside the bureaucratic organizing model and adopt customer-focused or customer-driven models in its place, the jobs become "enriched" without special attention. And, virtually every organization that has embraced worker teams and has empowered them to continuously improve quality or service or both, has experienced the incredible increase in motivation that Herzberg's research predicts.

If you're in a competitive industry, you'll know by your position in your marketplace.

Your customer relations will be extraordinary.

Your customers will have a special loyalty to you, earned because your products are at a quality level that is equal to or higher than they expect, and/or your customer service is dazzling.

Your customers will trust you more than they did before, and you'll be deserving that trust, because the people in your organization will care about your customers' interests as much as they care about your own.

Your customers may be more willing to consider a long-term relationship with your organization. Long-term relationships—as in the Japanese style—mean that your business relationship will have more stability.

Your market share will be growing or at least holding its own.

You will find that customers have a higher loyalty to your organization and will be less likely to leave your organization to go to a competitor.

In addition, you'll find that customer satisfaction brings referrals and new customers attracted by word of mouth.

Assuming that you stay up with or ahead of the other organizations in your market, who are also responding to the global emphasis on quality and customer service, you can expect your share of your market to grow.

Your margins will be increased considering your industry and your market positioning.

Assuming you aren't in a commodity business where quality or customer satisfaction are less important factors in customer repurchase tendencies, then you will find that extraordinary service quality is a very profitable strategy.

For those of you in truly competitive industries, where products or services can be differentiated in ways observable to customers, then you stand to gain greatly by achieving extraordinary service quality.

Consumers and business customers both have shown a greater willingness to pay a premium for product quality above expectations and for extraordinary levels of customer service.

So, in addition to gains in market share, you can measure the extent to which you have differentiated your organization from your competitors by the margins you are able to achieve.

If you're in government or a regulated monopoly, you'll know by how your stakeholders and your peers react toward you.

Your customer relations will be extraordinary.

There are fewer organizations in this category that are striving for extraordinary service quality, and customers also approach organizations like yours with lower expectations.

When government agencies or regulated monopolies become extraordinary in service quality, customers respond enthusiastically, and show a willingness to continue to be served by the organization.

Enthusiastic willingness to continue to be served translates into positive attitudes of customers and positive word-of-mouth comments, and may even result in political support for the organization.

Your customers will be easier to work with, more cooperative, more helpful and more patient.

You'll be a model for other organizations like yours.

You'll find that other organizations like yours will be coming for tours, presentations, and simply to find out how you did it. Your people will be asked to speak about your organization to association meetings. Your people will be in demand throughout your field as other organizations want to become more like you.

You'll find it easier to get the funding or rate hikes that you need.

There is a great likelihood that legislators, regulators or other stakeholders who influence your funding will be supportive of your needs. The public utilities and governmental agencies that are standouts today in terms of customer satisfaction tell me that it is still not easy to get needed funding increases and rate hikes. But, they also tell me confidentially that it's even harder for those agencies or utilities that aren't models for their industry.

You'll know by what has happened to your organizing form.

If your goal was to be "customer sensitive":

Your service quality improvement program was intended to improve your service quality, and still allow your organization to return to its traditional organizational form—the bureaucratic model.

You still have all of the attributes of the bureaucratic model:

a. **a formal hierarchy,** with each level managed by the level above.

b. **management by rules,** with every level controlled by rules set by levels higher in the organization.

c. **an in-focused (or up-focused) mission.** Your mission is to achieve profit, or growth, or market share, or funding, or some other goal that has value to the organization. Or, your mission is to serve the needs and purposes of some external stakeholders above the organization such as stockholders, or legislators.

d. **purposely impersonal.** The organization treats all employees the same, and all customers the same, without regard to their individual differences or personal needs.

e. **organized by function.** The organization organizes itself and its people into functional units based on the skills of the individuals or the function the individuals perform.

f. **hiring based on technical qualifications.** And, perhaps, protection from arbitrary termination.

The "shadow" organization that was established to improve service quality has done its work and has been dismantled. The organization has now returned to the "normal" way of operating, which has been sanctioned by time and tradition.

It is in the tradition of organizations based on the bureaucratic model to duck failure and to court success, so we can be certain that the service quality improvement campaign will have been deemed a great success. We can be confident that the scores for customer satisfaction will have been raised, and it will seem natural for the organization to go on to its "next" challenge.

If your goal was to be "customer focused":

You will have turned the traditional pyramid on its head, and the entire organization will be aligned around the mission of satisfying the customer. But, your organization will have divided into two distinctly different sub-organizations.

The portion of the organization closest to the customer will be organized into a permanent form of the "shadow organization." By that, we mean that most non-management people will be organized into action teams, guided by task forces, and trained and empowered to continuously improve service quality for internal and external customers.

The remainder of the organization will be organized as they have been traditionally. You'll have the same functional staff units and support units that you always had. You'll still have a goodly number of levels of managers, directors, vice presidents, senior vice presidents and so on. The functional units will be more supportive of the "shadow" organization and less controlling than they were before, but the functional units will still have the same "turf" interests and budget interests that have been by-products of the traditional organizing form.

Even though the two sub-organizations are aligned around the mission of customer satisfaction, the two organizations will have also become competitors for the traditional organizational perks. The formal and the shadow organization will compete for budget, for status, for influence with senior management, for their "programs" and for the "right" people for their organization. While each sub-organization will vie for dominance, neither can dominate because if it does, the organization will either be slipping back toward the traditional form, or forward toward the "customer driven" organizing form. Either shift would spell the death of the "customer-focused" goal state, and the resulting form would either be a reversion to the traditional organization with an in-focused mission, or a transition to a "customer-driven" organization with the gradual elimination of the traditional functional organization.

To resolve the tensions between the competing sub-organizations without reverting or transitioning, we can predict that the most common resolution will be more and more separation between the two organizations. It might be possible to make the "shadow" organization reasonably self-sufficient. It will be possible for the functional organization to co-exist with the shadow organization with an acceptable level of tension if:

- the shadow organization becomes highly autonomous
- the shadow organization evolves its own culture
- the links between the two organizations are formalized and governed by policies, practices and procedures that do not require flexibility or responsiveness on the part of the functional organization

If your goal was to be "customer driven":

You will find your organization to be completely transformed from the traditional organization that you had at the beginning.

Your formal organization will have gradually transitioned into the desired new form until eventually the existing functional organization virtually disappears. There may be a rudimentary staff left, who are clearly committed to the mission dictated by the stakeholders other than customers (such as stockholders, funding sources or legislators).

The flat, non-hierarchical structure of the shadow organization will now be the structure of the entire organization.

The organization won't be driven by rules. The mission will drive decisions, and people will be empowered with guidelines. When the guidelines work to achieve the desired service quality, then they will be used. When the guidelines don't achieve customer satisfaction, the people will be empowered to be flexible and use their judgment and experience to do what is required to satisfy customers.

The organization won't be purposely impersonal. Instead, the organization will have the requisite variety of responses to ensure that both employees and customers are treated as individuals, with unique needs and circumstances. This will not suggest that polices, practices and procedures will be implemented arbitrarily. It will mean that the organization offers enough choices and alternatives to its customers and employees so that each person can choose the solution he/she needs to match the unique situation.

The organization won't be organized functionally. Work units will be filled with every discipline or functional skill that will be needed to serve some group of customers (or some specific product) without having to cross any departmental boundaries to achieve their mission. Employees will no longer be loyal primarily to their discipline; instead their loyalty will be given to the team, their unique mission and their specific customers (or product).

And, it goes without saying that the mission of the entire organization is to satisfy, please, delight or even dazzle the customer. The goal and the primary measurement of the organization will be the extent to which customers are "loyal" to the organization. Or, for units of government and utilities with protected customer bases, the goal and primary measurement will be the extent to which customers are "willing to continue being served" by the organization.

To reach the state of being "customer driven" will be a long and challenging transformation. The transition will deeply affect employee satisfaction and loyalty, as well as customer satisfaction and loyalty. Many have begun on this path, and few have yet arrived to become models for us. There are currently as many paths as there are organizations aiming for transformation.

Those of us privileged to work with, and struggle along with, the pathfinders who are pioneering organizational transformation can testify to the challenge of the endeavor. We can also report the enormous satisfaction, pride, excitement and passion that is engendered by the journey.

Summary

• This chapter outlines how you'll know if you've realized your vision of your chosen goal state.

a. You'll know whether you've achieved your goal because the feedback you get from your customers and from your fellow employees will be different.

b. You'll know you've achieved your goal state because your people will be doing different things than they are doing in the bureaucratic organization.

c. Competitive organizations will know you've achieved your goal state because your customer relations, your market share and your margins will be significantly improved.

d. Governmental or regulated organizations will know you've achieved your chosen goal state based on how your stakeholders and peer organizations react to you.

e. You'll know by what has happened to your organizing form. If your goal was to be customer sensitive, you'll still be a bureaucracy, but your customer relations will be improved.

If your goal was to be customer focused, you'll have a customer-focused mission, but will still have the remaining vestiges of bureaucracy.

If your goal was to be customer driven, you'll have an organization perfectly attuned to your mission.

Many of the ideas and principles outlined in this book apply to government as well as the private sector

Preview

Some thoughts on how the ideas in this book could be applied to various levels of government. This section is not intended for people in government, but rather for people outside of government who might have an interest in seeing government become more effective.

This book has been aimed largely at executives operating in the private sector. Most of my research, data and experience has been in the private sector, and I am far more certain that the bureaucratic model is the wrong organizing model for private sector organizations than I am about government. There are people in government who remain certain that the bureaucratic model is the only possible way of organizing an agency or unit of government. Frankly, I have sincere doubts; however, there may be some agencies or units of government that have the courage to put aside some parts of the bureaucracy model and strive to be mission driven.

Citizens are increasingly frustrated with the poor results that governmental bureaucracies achieve on our critical social problems.

It doesn't take a keen observer to note that the typical citizen (in the United States) has little confidence that the governmental agencies are going to solve the critical social problems facing the country. The nation's problems with drugs, crime, poverty, welfare excesses, education, building and maintaining the infrastructure, energy dependence, the environment and more, are all in the hands of governmental agencies. Each of those agencies is organized and run based on the bureaucratic model.

In the past several years, my work has expanded to include state, provincial and national governments in the United States and Canada, with a dash of contact with agencies of government in France, England and Scotland as well. Close contact with people working in a variety of governmental agencies has helped me confront some of my prejudices. I confess that I formerly shared a number of prejudices with the average citizen towards governmental employees. I now know that governmental agencies are heavily populated with excellent people, most of whom care deeply about public service and about the critical issues that they deal with.

I am now even more convinced that the poor results that agencies of government produce cannot be blamed on the people in government, but instead on the organizational model that is used.

I discovered some excellent proof of this basic thesis when I read the work of Otto Brodtrick. Mr. Brodtrick identified eight of the best performing agencies in the Canadian government. In every instance, the agencies that were judged to be top-performing agencies had made one or more modifications to the basic bureaucratic model of organizing. Some took pains to be less hierarchical. Some empowered their front-line people. Some intentionally added back some "human" into their transactions. Virtually every one of the best-performing agencies changed the focus of their mission from being in-focused or up-focused, to being citizen focused or quality focused.

As a result of my work with government agencies, and becoming acquainted with people in government, I offer the following suggestions:

- Let's stop blaming the people in our public bureaucracies. Many good and caring people go into government and are eventually overwhelmed by the bureaucracy. It isn't the *people*—it's the organizing model.

- Let's also stop blaming the politicians. Most of them are attracted to government service because they really care and they want to make a difference in the world through public service. The reality is that any decisions that politicians make have to carried out by government workers immobilized by bureaucracy.

- The bureaucratic form puts great pressure on governmental agencies to be up-focused and in-focused, rather than customer focused. Agencies must first satisfy the legislators who bring them into being and are responsible for funding them. Once they satisfy the legislators, the organizing form next drives them to satisfy their own needs internally. Only then —if they have any energy or resources left—can they be concerned with satisfying their customers or achieving their external mission as the government employees themselves would like to do.

- The bureaucratic model fragments government into specialized agencies concerned only with their special interests.
  They aren't chartered to take a broad view, and sometimes
  aren't even allowed to. They have to encourage citizens to be
  concerned with their cause or they won't get funded. A very
  real problem for career government workers is that if they
  actually do solve their particular social problem, the need for
  the agency will disappear. So, in some cases, the self-interest
  of the agency can gradually become opposite that of the
  public.

- The hierarchical design of the bureaucracy model ensures
  that the people at the top will make the decisions. The result
  is the kind of central planning that almost single-handedly
  has been the downfall of state socialism and communism
  around the world. It is possible that this kind of central
  planning is necessary in the military and perhaps for a few
  other select agencies of government. But, I think it is equally
  clear that for many agencies of government, central planning
  and control doom their chances for success from the outset.

The bureaucratic form causes government agencies to become "top heavy" and "bottom lean."

The hierarchical design of the bureaucracy makes the typical agency
vulnerable to Parkinson's Law. This means the administrative and
management segment of the agency grows steadily over time, regardless of what happens to the operating segment (the lower
ranks) of the agency. As a result, I have observed that many bureaucratic organizations tend to grow "top heavy" and "bottom
lean." When budget squeezes come, agencies look first to save
money by cutting services at "the bottom" of the organization.

Governmental agencies cut services at the bottom of the organization for two reasons. First, it's those people near the top of the
organization who decide who gets cut. Second, if the agency does
serve customers (or provides a needed service), the taxpayers will
feel "the pinch" more by cuts near the bottom of the organization,
and may be more responsive to appeals for more money.

For example, a major city ordered percentage cuts across the board in all agencies. In virtually every department, the agencies made the bulk of their cuts in the lower levels of the agency. Particularly noticeable were the fire department and the police department, where the cuts were made in front-line people, and the "top heavy" ranks were scarcely touched. The agency's self interests were best served by reducing services, thus putting the maximum possible imposition on the citizens—in hopes that the citizens would demand that their particular budgets be restored.

Another example: in October 1990, the U.S. Congress, the president and his administration were racing to agree on a deficit reduction plan before the Gramm-Rudman-Hollings Act would force automatic, across-the-board cuts. On Tuesday, October 9, the federal government would be forced to implement huge cuts unless Congress and the president agreed on a new budget over the long holiday weekend.

The governmental agency that governs public lands and parks, closed national parks and monuments to tourists on October 6, 7, and 8. One can only speculate that the purpose was to disappoint and frustrate citizens as visibly and obviously as possible as a way of focusing attention on what the people would lose if government budgets were cut.

Taxpayers, legislators and the media will not succeed in cutting waste and bloat in government as long as cuts are administered more heavily on the lower ranks of governmental agencies than on the upper ranks. This is not something that can be blamed on the individuals who work for the agencies. Actually, in terms of the "game" that people feel forced to play when they work for a full-fledged bureaucracy, they are playing the game correctly. Because the mission of any given bureaucratic agency is sub-optimal and focused very narrowly, it isn't the job of the people in any given agency to see to the larger, overall mission of good government, or social order or building for the future.

What might change in government if it could put aside the bureaucratic organizing model?

Suppose, for a moment, that agencies were not focused so narrowly on their tiny spectrum of social problems. Suppose, for example, that it were possible to focus on outcomes and not processes, and that individual agencies were required to "nest" their missions within a larger state-wide, province-wide, or nation-wide mission.

A whimsical example: suppose the U.S. Department of Justice, which is concerned with law enforcement and maintaining the prison system, got together with the State Department, which is responsible for considering the needs of neighboring nations. Sprinkle in some creativity and the U.S. Congress might be considering legislation to allow other countries to bid on housing our "career" criminals (those willing to forfeit their rights to constitutional protection by committing three or more felonies.) Jailing our "career" criminals in Mexico, San Salvador or Panama would benefit those countries by infusing capital for construction of jails, and jobs for citizens from those countries as jailors, cooks, wardens, etc. At the same time, politicians would not have to struggle with voters who don't want more prisons in their neighborhoods. And, to top it all off, by accepting the lowest bidders, we could house our criminals much more cheaply than we do currently.

More whimsy: suppose the people responsible for welfare, who are concerned with providing for the poor and homeless, got together with the State Department. We might achieve what many have so long yearned for—the ability to make poor people affluent. At some point in the welfare cycle, if an individual gives up hope or stops trying to be self-sufficient, then that person could be put on a pension (at much less than it costs to keep that person on welfare in the United States), in Bolivia, Peru, or Haiti, or other nations where an amount that would keep them in poverty in the United States would allow them to live very well.

This would stimulate the economy of those nations, create service jobs, and from some viewpoints, it could be said that "everybody wins." The proverbial "welfare mother" that so infuriates conservatives could, at a lower cost than present welfare costs, have a relatively luxurious home in other nearby nations.

These whimsical notions are not presented as serious proposals. They are offered as examples of what "synergy" becomes possible when you step out of the bureaucratic box of looking only at one problem at a time.

Some less whimsical observations

In any given agency (given their in-focused and sub-optimal mission), their first responsibility is to survive and grow in order to apply more resources to the "process" of working on a given social issue.

- The bureaucratic focus on rules instead of mission achievement causes the red tape that citizens and businesses find so frustrating and wasteful. It often happens that the people in government are forced to follow rules that get in the way of achieving the mission.

Governmental agencies are typically formed by legislators, through legislation, and thus are born through "laws," which are the toughest form of "rules." As a consequence, agencies typically don't have as much choice about turning "rules" into "guidelines," which can be put aside when they interfere with the agency's mission. This means that most government agencies feel forced to follow their "rules" even though the people involved may be fully aware that the "rules" do not result in achieving the "mission."

- The impersonal design goal of bureaucracy results in good, caring people being forced to behave in ways that seem cold and uncaring.

Governmental agencies are generally perceived by citizen "customers" as being really terrible at providing service or producing customer satisfaction. Governmental agencies are essentially forced to be "purposely impersonal." The idea behind being purposely impersonal is well meaning. The intention is to ensure that all people are treated equally, and the rich don't get better treatment than the poor, and that people with influence or social standing don't get better treatment than the ordinary citizen.

The unfortunate part is the choice of strategy. Many governmental agencies are forced to give everyone the same treatment without regard to race, religion, sex, age or affluence. It is unfortunate that the principles of the bureaucratic organizing model causes the agencies to strive for equal treatment rather than equal satisfaction.

Having spent most of this book advising senior managers in the private sector to transform their organizations, I suppose it's even more grandiose to suggest that I might have a formula for reforming government as well. On the other hand, if I'm right about how the bureaucratic organizing model causes so many problems in the private sector, I think it's valuable to at least consider that it may be doing the same thing in the public sector.

Idea #1: For service agencies, one strategy would be to use the bureaucratic process itself to reduce the negative effects of bureaucracy on the citizenry.

- For example, we could ask legislators to pass regulations linking agency funding with citizen satisfaction ratings. This would help governmental agencies balance their up-focus with a customer focus. The people in those agencies would welcome our support and appreciate our help in giving them a clear charter to satisfy customers. In addition, the agencies would then have a clear mandate to collect customer feedback, which they could use to drive higher and higher satisfaction scores.

- We could ask legislators to pass regulations requiring that budget cuts impact first above the line, and last below the line. This would keep agencies from becoming "top heavy, bottom lean, or better yet, it might totally erase the line.

Idea #2: Let's give the governmental bureaucracies more competition from non-profit organizations and private enterprise. This will help them become less in-focused and more customer focused. It's easier to stay mission driven—and harder to fall back into bureaucratic ways—when competitive forces are at work.

- Let's give private enterprise a chance at the kids that public education has given up on. And if the private sector produces good results, let's install their products in our public schools. If we are truly going to achieve our ambitions for our children, we have to help our long-suffering, under-appreciated teachers and administrators overcome the immobilizing effects of bureaucracy.

- Let's privatize more of the functions now handled by agencies of government. If we have to involve government, let government oversee things rather than actually do the work whenever possible.

As we privatize, let's make sure that we relax the grip that bureaucracy has on the privatized organizations. For example, the United States has had both public and private schools for a long time. If you ask private schools, however, they'll tell you that they have to conform to many, if not all, of the same "rules" and suffocating structure that have immobilized public education. To be accredited and to have grades and transcripts accepted by other institutions, private schools are forced to accommodate their curricula and instructional processes to suit the public educational bureaucracy's norms.

Some observers argue that privatization doesn't always work to produce market sensitivity and effectiveness in organizations that once were run by government. I suggest that we look carefully at each case to see if the bureaucratic controls were lifted along with privatization, and if the organization was allowed to shift from a bureaucratic organization to a mission-driven organization.

Private ownership, by itself, only adds additional pressure for profitability to a formerly governmental organization, which can be just another way of producing an up-focused or in-focused mission. To achieve its full potential, privatized organizations must be given some flexibility, or else they will succumb to the same bureaucratic immobilization that afflicts many governmental agencies.

For example, private waste management has spread across the country, providing superior service at a lower cost than waste management provided by local governments.

Another example: private prisons are being considered throughout the United States. I think it is fair to say that so far, bureaucracies have not had much success in reducing either drug abuse or poverty. As a consequence, U.S. prisons are overflowing, and with little citizen support for more investment in prisons, private prisons are being considered and adopted more often. If private prisons are given some flexibility, they may innovate some new strategies that both incarcerate and rehabilitate prisoners more effectively than the public prison system does. If private prisons are suffocated by the same bureaucratic "rule book" that causes public prisons to be ineffectual, then private prisons can only live up to part of their potential.

Idea #3: Let's stop turning our problems over to government if it is going to try to solve them through bureaucratic processes.

- For example, the solution to the "drug problem" is not further escalating the drug war. Bureaucracies are limited to a few processes and are process driven rather than results driven. The bureaucratic solutions to the drug problem seem to be narrowed down to either escalation of the drug war or de-criminalization of drugs. Non-bureaucratic thinkers have suggested that the optimal answer may lie between the two bureaucratic solutions.

- Another example: few people think that the U.S. government's Veterans Administration runs better hospitals or gives veterans better care than they could receive from the "normal" doctors and hospitals. For less tax money, it's highly probable that we could give the veterans better care with less bureaucratic red tape than they get from the Veterans Administration.

Idea #4: We could go all the way, and help government agencies adopt a new model to replace the bureaucratic model. I suggest we not define the "process," but rather define the outcomes we want. We could evaluate our agencies using "Malcolm Baldrige Award" type criteria, and allocate resources based on success in meeting the criteria.

- We could ask our lawmakers to pass legislation creating "replacement" agencies, organized on the non-bureaucratic model. The lawmakers could then transfer the burdens away from our most immobilized bureaucracies to the replacement agencies.

  We would then find out if new agencies, organized in a different way, can't do a better job for the citizenry. Remember, it isn't the people in government, it's the organizing model. I've seen people hired into my company, who have worked in bureaucratic organizations for years, put bureaucratic behaviors aside and become "mission driven" almost overnight.

Appendix II

The Shadow Organization

Preview

This section offers more details and more examples regarding "shadow organizations." This section will be most valuable to people who will be responsible for implementing organizational change. It is also designed to help senior executives think through how they might set up a shadow organization to match their chosen goal state.

Introduction

This document's purpose is to acquaint you with some of the ways in which a shadow organization is different from the traditional organization.

The term "shadow organization" refers to a second organizational structure imposed upon an existing organization. Sometimes, the second organizational structure is called an "informal" organization, imposed upon the "formal" organization. You may also hear it called a "parallel" organization.

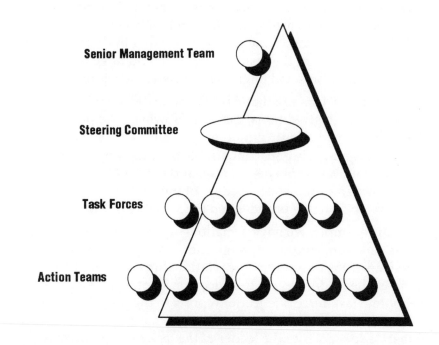

The structure of the shadow organization

The chart above is an example of how a shadow organization might be organized. The chart illustrates a senior management team, one steering committee, six or more task forces and a number of action teams.

The rest of this appendix shows how one shadow organization might be put together. However, there is no standard. Each organization will decide to structure their shadow organization the way that best suits their particular situation and culture.

To illustrate, imagine a normal, traditional organization. It is managed in a hierarchical manner, with each level controlling those levels below it and being controlled by the levels above. Now, if we took a group of middle managers from the various functional units in the traditional organization and assigned them roles in a task force, we are creating a second organization on top of the base organization.

When the people in the task force are doing their regular jobs, their reporting relationships are clear and their level of authority is also clear. When those same people are acting in their secondary roles, as members of the task force, they could have different reporting relationships and might have different levels of authority.

For example, let's say that ABC Company is organized in functional units in the traditional manner. However, the president becomes concerned about "employee morale," an issue that needs work across multiple departments. So, the president names a task force to work on employee morale, and calls it the "morale task force." He names someone "leader" of the task force, and asks the leader to report to the president on the activities of the task force.

In this example, we have a shadow organization being formed out of, and superimposed upon, the existing organization. The leader now has two reporting relationships. During normal situations, the leader reports to a vice president. On the activities of the morale task force, the leader reports to the president. Each of the members normally reports to different managers, and now each of them also reports to the leader of the task force for activities relating to the morale task force.

In this example, we call the morale task force a "cross-functional" task force because it brings people together from a variety of functional units. If the president had picked the team from all the people in one branch office, we would call the team a "natural work unit" task force. Multi-disciplinary teams (another term that we use), describes multiple disciplines that could be either from one functional unit or from several functional units.

For example, a management information systems department might have several sections organized by discipline: the programming section, the operators' section, the systems section, the data base section, etc. If the MIS department formed a task force with a member from each section, that team could be called multidisciplinary, even though it represents only one function within the organization—MIS.

Organizations form task forces or steering committees frequently, and they don't think too much about it. Task forces are set up, they do a job, and then they disappear. People don't make much of it, nor do they get confused by it.

Why task forces and other shadow units are needed

Organizations using the bureaucratic organizing model find it difficult to change. Organizing people functionally, by their work specialty, training or background, results in a set of functional units, each of which have their own in-focused goals, objectives and perhaps their own missions. Over time, these functional units regulate each others' roles and expansion. There is a kind of tension existing between functional units that keeps any one unit from growing more rapidly than, or at the expense of, other functional units.

The self-regulation, or natural tension, that exists between functional units results in "stasis," or exceptional stability. Any change that would significantly affect the delicate balance between functional units is resisted by all functional units that might possibly be affected by the change.

As a result of the exceptional stability, the dynamics of any bureaucratic organization result in resistance to significant changes. Small changes are allowed and accepted as normal. Significant or meaningful changes are resisted. A change in mission is such a significant change that the bureaucratic organization probably couldn't achieve it without some help.

A shadow organization is a second, separate organization, superimposed upon the primary organization, that can achieve significant change. The effect of the shadow organization is to work around the stabilizing force of the functional units in stasis and introduce changes that the functional organization is better able to accept.

So, if executives in a bureaucratic organization seek to make any significant change in the status quo, a shadow organization is very useful to achieve the change.

The power of the shadow organization

The power of the shadow organization is its elasticity, flexibility, changeability and somewhat ethereal nature.

A task force by its nature is elastic, flexible, changeable and ethereal. It can be formed easily and it can disappear just as easily. It can be elastic in size, growing and shrinking as various skills are added or deleted from it. The charter of the task force can be changed, modified, flexed or even totally eliminated.

A task force exists at the will of the individuals who formed it and empowered it. A task force is as powerful as its sponsors and its charter permit it to be.

Traditional bureaucratic organizations are typically permanent and unable to change; shadow organizations have the power to produce change, but (within traditional bureaucratic organizations) are typically not permanent.

Using a shadow organization for large-scale change

When an organization undertakes to make a significant change, either in its mission, vision or strategy, it is sometimes necessary to form a large number of shadow units, which all work together to achieve the change.

For example, let's say that the president of XYZ Company decides to change the organization's basic mission, vision and strategy, and create a "customer-focused" organization, with a customer-focused mission, vision and strategy. This kind of change, one that affects the entire organization, is too much for one task force, or one steering committee, working alone. So, the following units are formed to work on this change:

(1) Senior management team

(1) Steering committee to manage the transition

(6) Task forces to link with the existing functional units

(37) Action teams, to manage various assignments during the transition.

When you introduce more than a few shadow units—and you link them together—you are essentially creating an entire second level of the organization, superimposed upon the first. This second level of organization is what we are talking about when we use the term "shadow" organization.

Purpose of the shadow organization.

The purpose of the shadow organization, within any given organization, will depend on the goal that the functional organization wants to achieve. The design of the shadow organization depends on the goal you choose.

To illustrate, let's examine three possible goal states that an organization might choose. We have arbitrarily assigned these three goal states names that are sometimes used interchangeably: "customer sensitive," "customer focused," and "customer driven."

Purpose, makeup and duration of a shadow organization in a "customer sensitive" organization.

We define a "customer-sensitive" organization as one that seeks to maintain its existing organizational form, and yet seeks improved service quality.

Purpose of the shadow organization

Given the goal of maintaining the existing organization, the shadow organization's purpose will be to come into existence, improve service quality, and then disappear.

Makeup

Given the desire to maintain the existing organization, and use the shadow organization as a method for achieving change, it makes sense to make all shadow organization roles temporary. One way to do this is to consider these assignments as temporary, and rotate people through the shadow organization and then back to a job in the functional organization. Another approach is to make all of the assignments part time, and ask people to take on steering committee, task force or action team assignments in addition to their regular roles.

Considering that the shadow organization will eventually disappear, people will naturally avoid permanent assignment to the shadow organization for fear of being caught without a chair when the music stops.

Duration and future

Given the goal state of maintaining the existing organization—while bringing service quality up to customer expectations—the duration of the shadow organization may be fairly short. The future lies with the existing organization, and the duration of the shadow organization is uncertain.

The shadow organization could disappear in a variety of scenarios. The best scenario would be that service quality goals would be achieved and the shadow organization would be dismantled thoughtfully. Less promising scenarios could see the end of the shadow organization because of any of the following reasons:

- An unexpected budget crunch
- A change in senior management, e.g., a new CEO
- Tension between the shadow and functional organizations
- Shadow organization people stressed by handling two jobs
- New issues taking precedence over service quality improvement
- Outside stakeholders (boards, or legislators) changing priorities

Purpose, makeup and duration of a shadow organization in a "customer-focused" organization.

We define a "customer-focused" organization as one with a customer-focused mission, but which otherwise maintains a traditional organizational form. This goal state is chosen by organizations seeking extraordinary service quality.

Purpose

The purpose of the shadow organization will be to co-exist permanently with the functional organization. The shadow organization will gradually take over all customer contact or product quality responsibility. The challenge is to make sure that the functional organization doesn't get in the way of the customer-focused mission.

The inclination of the functional part of the organization will be to set up barriers to customer satisfaction through its in-focused goals and activities. On the other hand, the shadow organization must take care that it doesn't "flaunt" its new culture, values or mission as superior to that of the functional organization.

Makeup

Given the goal of converting to a customer-focused mission (while maintaining the rest of the existing organization), it makes sense to make some of the steering committee and task force assignments full-time permanent jobs. It also makes sense to staff the shadow organization with "fast track" management talent who have the potential to become senior management within the functional organization. This strategy makes it possible that future senior managers may be people with strong commitment to a customer-focused mission.

The use of action teams (made up of non-management people) will probably be a permanent change in the way that the functional organization operates. If this is anticipated, then it makes sense to use functional supervisors in new roles as facilitators and coaches of the action teams. This will encourage supervisors to coach rather than discipline.

Duration and future

Given the goal of a permanent change to a customer-focused mission, the future of the shadow organization is more secure than it is with organizations seeking to maintain their existing organizations and their in-focused missions.

The idea is to maintain a permanent shadow organization that will continuously improve service quality far into the future. The shadow organization will evolve its own culture and method of operation. To achieve its goals, the shadow organization will need to be different from the functional organization in many ways. The shadow organization will evolve away from rigid hierarchy, and use empowerment as the norm.

Rules will be relaxed somewhat and become guidelines that are put aside when they interfere with the mission. The human component of interpersonal relations will be added in both internal and external customer transactions. And, the shadow organization will have as much cross-functional and multi-disciplinary teaming as needed to overcome the bureaucratic barriers that exist within the functional organization.

It is important to understand that the functional and shadow organizations will be in some conflict from the beginning. As the shadow organization strengthens and produces successes, the tension between the two sub-organizations will build. This tension can be managed and competitiveness can be reduced with pre-planning, training and understanding.

The more the two sub-organizations become aligned around the customer-focused mission, the less conflict will be produced. The more the two sub-organizations can be measured by the same measurements, the less conflict will be produced. This probably will mean that traditional productivity measurements will have to be downplayed, and customer satisfaction measurements will have to be reinforced for the functional organization.

Purpose, makeup and duration of a "customer-driven" organization

We define a "customer-driven" organization as one that is willing to adopt whatever organizational form is needed to achieve extraordinary customer relations.

Purpose

Given the goal of creating the optimal organization for achieving extraordinary customer relations, the purpose of the shadow organization is to be a catalyst to eventually transform the existing organization. The goal here is to install a new culture and a new way of organizing, managing and operating that are totally customer driven. In this case, the existing functional organization will not permanently coexist with the new organization; it will gradually be transformed into a new organization and the traditional functional organization will disappear.

Makeup

Given the goal of transforming the existing functional organization into a new organizational form designed specifically to achieve extraordinary customer relations, the shadow organization needs to be selected most carefully. In this situation, you want your very best people to create the shadow organization, and to build the shadow organization to such a level of strength, talent, and commitment that it will stand as a skeleton onto which the remainder of the functional organization gradually can be built.

The shadow organization will be made up largely of permanent assignments (at least at the steering committee and task force level), and people will be selected more by their aptitude for the new organizational form than by their effectiveness in mastering the traditional organizational form.

Duration and future

Given the goal of replacing the existing organization over time with a new organizational form, culture, management style and ways of operating and organizing, the shadow organization will be the training ground and development base for the future organization. Everything that the people who populate the shadow organization learn will be valued skills in the transformed organization. In most ways the transformed organization will have attributes identical to those of the units in the shadow organization.

Culture of the shadow organization

Depending upon the goal state, the desired culture in the shadow organization will vary. If the goal is to be a customer-sensitive organization, then the culture of the shadow organization will largely reflect that of the functional organization. One exception will be in the expected cooperation and collaboration between team members. Whereas it might be accepted behavior in the functional organization for people in different units to be uncooperative and even competitive, the behavior of people in the shadow organization will need to be collaborative.

In situations where the goal state is customer focused or customer driven, it is very important to purposely manage the culture of the shadow organization. The culture of the shadow organization needs to be less hierarchical and more attuned to empowerment; less concerned with rules and more with the mission; less concerned with process and more concerned with outcomes; more human, personal, and concerned with individual needs and less with the formal application of procedures or policies.

The culture in the shadow organization may be managed in a variety of ways. The culture can be managed by a task force, the steering committee, or through the training of all members of the shadow organization.

Responsiveness of the shadow organization

Regardless of the goal state, the shadow organization needs to have responsiveness standards far different from the underlying functional organization.

One of the major problems with the hierarchical, functional and impersonal nature of the bureaucratic organizing form is that it is slow to respond. The more bureaucratic the organization, the slower the response time. So, the shadow organization must—from the beginning—set new standards for responsiveness that will allow progress to be achieved.

For example, in one organization that functioned so slowly its people described it as "glacial," the following new standards for interactions between shadow units were set:

- Requests from action teams to task forces would be responded to within 72 hours. If no response was received within 72 hours, the action team could consider their recommendation or request approved.

- Requests from task forces to the steering committee could expect a response within 72 hours. If no response was received within 72 hours, the task force could consider their recommendation or request approved.

- Requests from the steering committee to the senior management team could expect an answer with 48 hours. If they did not receive an answer within 48 hours, they were to consider the request approved.

By installing the automatic approval, the organization provided consequences for delays that would be inevitable if there were no consequences.

Action teams: natural work units, cross-functional, or multi-disciplinary in makeup.

Whether a temporary and part-time activity, or a permanent and full-time way of operating, all action teams will use team skills and teamwork to continuously improve service quality.

The role of action teams

Action teams (or service quality teams, or whatever you choose to call them) are groups of employee—typically non-management people—who meet regularly to manage specific "moments of truth" for external and internal customers. The moment of truth to be managed might be assigned by the service quality task force (to be described later in this paper), or selected by the action team and cleared with the SQ task force, to ensure that other teams aren't working on the same moment of truth. Activities of the action teams (in our example), would:

- Analyze a specific cycle of service.

  A "cycle of service" analysis is a method of examining a service from the viewpoint of the customer. The service cycle is broken down into "moments of truth," which are defined as "opportunities for customers to form loyalty, generating an impression of the organization's service." For example, in the service cycle for a bank's retail checking account service, we would find a moment of truth called "opening a checking account" on the service cycle. We would probably not find a moment of truth called "noticing the color of paint on the lobby walls." It's not that paint colors aren't important, it's simply that they are not likely to affect very many customers' decisions about staying loyal to this bank.

- Determine the impact of the moment of truth on customer satisfaction or loyalty.

  In any given service cycle, some moments of truth will be memorable to the customer long after the service is rendered, and some will not. The idea here is to identify those moments of truth that are most likely to be part of a customer's decision about being willing to continue being served by this organization (customer loyalty).

- Determine the current degree of customer satisfaction.

  The action teams will gather what is known about current customer satisfaction with each of the potentially impression-forming moments of truth in the service cycle. There may or may not be research available. If there is no formal research, the team may use input from front-line employees (or themselves) as proxies for input from customers themselves. (This is not too risky during the selection stage of the process.)

- Select (or be assigned) the moment of truth with the highest potential impact on customer satisfaction and loyalty.

- Gather the data on customer expectations (if it doesn't already exist); gather the data on customer satisfaction (if it doesn't already exist); examine the data to pinpoint the reasons for current customer dissatisfaction.

- Examine the moment of truth for opportunities to enrich the service delivery with service skills known to be associated with increasing customer loyalty.

- Select and plan to install the service skills that will have the highest potential impact on customer satisfaction and loyalty.

- Implement the solution to the non-conformance and add the service enhancers and recovery strategies. Monitor customer satisfaction with the moment of truth. Work iteratively through the process until the fixes and the service enhancers produce the desired level of customer satisfaction.

- Feed forward the new method of managing the moment of truth to all service delivery units that interact with customers on that moment of truth.

- Collect possible causes for non-conformance to customer expectations (or standards) and determine the "root cause" of the non-conformance.

- Brainstorm possible solutions to the root cause, and perform a cost/benefit analysis of possible solutions.

- Select the optimal solution to the non-conformance.

- Celebrate the success of the project, recognize those who contributed, and employ other tangible or intangible rewards for the team members and other contributors.

- Go back to the beginning and start over on a new moment of truth, or another problem associated with the original moment of truth.

Inputs to action teams

- **From the training task force**

  The action teams need to be trained how to work as teams; to be committed to and even "passionate" about service quality; and to understand the process of continuous improvement itself (how to manage moments of truth to achieve increased customer loyalty).

- **From the SQ (service quality) task force**

  The SQ task force assigns some of the customer moments of truth to be managed by action teams. In addition, the SQ task force serves a clearing function for the action teams. This clearing function ensures that two action teams aren't working on the same moment of truth at the same time.

  The SQ task force also provides expertise in work processes and work re-design to action teams when they need help.

- **From the measurement task force**

  The action team will receive any existing customer satisfaction research that pertains to the service cycle the team is analyzing.

  Upon request from the action team, the measurement task force will either do a baseline measurement of customer satisfaction with the selected moment of truth the team has chosen, or train and empower team members to do so.

  When the fixes and enhancers are added, the measurement task force will either do continuous measurement of that moment of truth to measure the change from the baseline, or the measurement task force may train the team to conduct such measurements.

After the fixes and enhancements have been fed forward to all customer contact sites for the selected moment of truth, the measurement task force will see that periodic monitoring is done to ensure that the fixes and enhancers are holding up over time.

- **From employees who contact these customers**

    The action team will solicit input from employees who currently implement the moment of truth. This may supplement or take the place of input from a measurement task force.

- **From customers**

    Some action teams may be empowered to conduct interviews, focus panels, surveys, or collect critical-incident stories from customers directly about their current experience with the moment of truth, or their expectations about that moment of truth, or about proposed fixes and enhancers before they are implemented.

    The need for the action team to do this customer satisfaction work themselves will depend on the availability and accessibility of the measurement task force and the training and capabilities of those on the action team. If numerous action teams are empowered to do direct research with customers, some coordination will be needed to avoid contacting the same customer by several different teams.

- **From the communications task force**

    The communications task force will provide the action team with unvarnished feedback about the experiences of other action teams. The goal will be to help action teams learn from each others' positive, negative, and neutral experiences.

    The communications task force will play a role in feeding forward new policies, practices and procedures as they are changed by the activities of the action teams. It will also play a role in recognizing successes of action teams and celebrating the improvements in customer satisfaction.

- **From supervisors in the functional organization**

    Supervisors will support the activities of the action teams by making time and support available to members whose activities might be a burden to the normal activities of the functional units.

Supervisors who coach, model and support the action team activities give the action teams permission and protection to pursue improved service quality.

- **From the steering committee**

The steering committee feeds information and encouragement to the action teams as needed.

The steering committee plays an important part in celebrating action team successes and recognizing innovation, creativity and extra effort when observed in action teams. The steering committee can play another supportive role by sharing reports on customer satisfaction improvements designed for the senior management team—with every level in the shadow organization, including action teams.

- **From the senior management team**

The senior management team provides the action teams with support and reinforcement. They will provide this support through their communications about the mission, the strategy, the vision and the goals for customer satisfaction.

The senior management team can be supportive by modeling concern for customer satisfaction in every decision, talk, statement and meeting.

Outputs from action teams

- Progress reports to the SQ task force. The SQ task force (if there is one) may request progress reports from each action team.
- Requests for clearance to work on the chosen MOT. If the moment of truth was not assigned, but was chosen by the action team, then clearance to work on that MOT will be needed. This avoids having more than one action team working on the same MOT.
- Requests for consulting help from the SQ task force if needed. In situations where the root cause of customer dissatisfaction is the design of the process—and the action team doesn't have any members capable of process redesign—then the action team will need help from those with advanced training on the SQ task force.

- Requests for existing data from the measurement task force on expectations and current levels of customer satisfaction.

- Requests to the measurement task force for continuous monitoring during installation of the proposed fixes and enhancers.

- Requests to the SQ task force, upon successful completion of tests of the fixes and enhancers, for approval, to feed forward the fix to all units that participate in the delivery of that moment of truth to customers.

- Requests to the PPP task force (policies, practices and procedures) for revisions as needed to make the PPPs "customer friendly." In moments of truth that require revised policies, practices, or procedures, either to "fix" the problem or to "enhance" customer satisfaction, the action team will propose possible revisions to the PPP task force.

Task forces

Task forces will typically be staffed by managers from several different functional areas. The task force will be responsible for the link between a specific functional unit and the shadow organization (except for domains where no functional unit may currently exist, such as customer satisfaction measurement and service quality.) Managers serving on task forces must be capable of bridging the different cultures and practices that will exist in the shadow organization and the functional organization.

The purpose of the task forces is to align the functional organization with the service quality mission and strategies of the shadow organization. The reason for the cross-cultural makeup of the task force is to stimulate new behaviors in the functional unit, rather than risk the in-focused, defensive ("everything we are currently doing is correct and the shadow organization is making unreasonable demands") reactions that can occur if the task force is made up solely of people from the functional unit involved.

The role of the communications task force

The role is to clarify and align all top-down communications with the service quality thrust. In addition, the role is to facilitate increased communication from employees throughout the functional and shadow organizations.

The task force will be responsible for monitoring and changing all communications (top-down, divisional, functional, etc.) within the organization and to the external customer, to make communications customer focused and forthright.

Inputs

• *From action teams*

Action teams will give the communications task force input on their activities, their successes, their failures, and what they tried that had no impact.

• *From other task forces*

Each task force will feed input to the communications task force so their activities can be communicated, along with their successes and failures.

• *From the steering committee*

The steering committee will provide input on the charter, the mission, the current state of customer satisfaction, the strategy for change, and feedback the steering committee has received from task forces.

• *From senior management*

Senior management will give the communications task force access to it, and will give input on their perception of the progress of the overall customer satisfaction effort.

Senior management will provide clear statements of intention about its commitment to the change effort, and the intended duration of the shadow organization. Senior management will give periodic updates on each of these points.

• *From people in the functional organization*

People in the functional organization (but not involved in shadow units), will provide input about their reaction to the service quality effort and its impact on their work, work load, and work attitudes.

Outputs

- "Straight talk" communication to all units of the shadow organization about the status and progress of the service quality improvement effort.

  "Straight talk" is a little-known form of communication in bureaucratic organizations. The idea of straight talk is to "tell it like it is," without any attempt to put "spin" on internal communications. Bureaucracies often distort internal communications to show events or issues in their most positive light. The purpose of straight talk to is to rebuild credibility in the organization, in management and in the accuracy of internal communications.

- Celebration and recognition when a MOT is being managed, so as to achieve the desired goal of rewarding good performance, customer satisfaction and improved customer loyalty.

- Communication with people throughout the functional organization to keep them informed of the project, report on stresses and challenges between the shadow and the functional unit, and update everyone on the remaining duration of the effort and timetables of projects still being planned.

The role of the training task force

The training task force evaluates all existing training programs for alignment with the organizational mission and goal state.

It responds to training needs identified and surfaced by action teams managing moments of truth.

Inputs

- Feedback from trainees on customer reactions and satisfaction levels with the existing system.

- Feedback from the action teams on additional training needed to better manage moments of truth.

- Feedback from the measurement task force on customer satisfaction with customer-contact employees.

Outputs

- Feedback to the measurement task force on information collected from trainees on customer reactions and satisfaction levels within the existing system.
- Recommendations to the steering committee for new, revised, or improved training programs and strategies that will accelerate the improvement of service quality.

The role of the measurement task force

The measurement task force develops new measurement and feedback systems to support the SQ effort. In addition, this task force collects information from all sources relating to customer satisfaction, expectations, and loyalty, and makes it available to action teams or task forces working to improve service quality.

A second, but equally important role, is to identify existing measurements that drive behaviors that negate efforts to improve service quality or result in goal displacement, and to withdraw these or remove their consequences.

Inputs

- Research on customer expectations about specific moments of truth.
- Feedback from customers on overall satisfaction.
- Feedback from customers on satisfaction with a specific MOT.
- Customer feedback passed on by direct customer contact people.
- Customer feedback from complaints and compliments.
- Feedback from customers on their reactions to proposed new approaches to high-impact MOTs.
- Benchmark information on competitors and "best-in-class" organizations.
- Indirect customer feedback collected through legislators, regulators, consumer advocates, etc.

Outputs

- Pass on customer feedback relating to service providers directly to the individual or team of service providers involved.

- Pass on customer feedback relating to policies, practices and procedures to the PPP task force, and keep in a data base for task teams managing affected MOTs.

- Pass on customer feedback relating to product or service quality, or value to SQ task force, and keep it available for task teams managing affected MOTs.

- Pass on to the steering committee the scores on overall satisfaction and score changes for MOTs being managed.

- Pass on to the steering committee summaries of customer feedback, as well as unedited samples of raw customer feedback.

The role of the performance management task force

The role of the performance management task force is to align the organization's performance management system with the organization's goal state and mission. If the desired goal state dictates a permanent change in the mission and organization, then the appraisal system, the rewards and recognition systems, and the promotion system will have to be temporarily or permanently changed.

Inputs

- The desired goal state from senior management.

- The desired rate of change, and the duration and the permanence of the desired changes, from the steering committee.

- Feedback on the existing performance management system from employees to clarify what behaviors and performance the existing system is producing.

Outputs

- Changes in the present employee appraisal system to align with the chosen goal state and mission.

- Changes in the salary administration plan so that it rewards employees who align with the organization's chosen mission and goal state.

- Changes in the promotion system in the functional organization. Depending on the goal state, the task force could establish a system for employee growth and achievement that relies less on promotions between hierarchical levels and more on contributions to team efforts at service quality improvement.

The role of the service quality task force

The SQ task force is responsible for causing high impact moments of truth to be managed, and supporting the action teams that manage each moment of truth. An important support role is to provide consulting or facilitation to action teams that need skills more advanced than are available within each team, e.g., process re-design, process control, etc.

It is possible that there is no corresponding functional unit in the functional organization. In those cases, this task force will have to identify those functional units with which liaison will be needed.

Depending upon the chosen goal state and mission, this task force may play a role in sponsoring the reorganization of the functional organization to clarify the responsibilities for quality and value of products and services.

Inputs

- Requests from action teams for clearance to manage their selected highest impact MOTs.
- Requests for consultation or facilitation in advanced skills not contained within the team.
- Customer feedback from the measurement task force on issues relating to quality or value of products or services.
- Changes in policies, practices and procedures from the PPP task force that will impact the quality and value of products and services delivered to customers.
- Approval, as needed, from the steering committee to delegate responsibilities to specific task teams which ordinarily would fall within the turf of a functional unit in the functional organization.
- Requests from action teams to feed forward fixes and enhancements that have been successfully piloted to the necessary service delivery units of the functional organization.

Outputs

- Formation of cross-functional action teams as needed to handle high impact MOTs that require cross-functional cooperation.

- Formation of multi-disciplinary action teams as needed to handle moments of truth that require several disciplines to support.

- Assignment of moments of truth to be managed by action teams.

- Approval for natural work unit action teams to manage MOTs that they have selected that are not being managed by any other action team.

- Requests to the steering committee for additional resources or budget allocation, where needed, to improve customer satisfaction or build loyalty on high impact MOTs.

- Authorization to action teams, where needed, to pursue fixes and enhancements that they would not ordinarily be authorized to use (within the functional organization).

- Consulting and facilitation as needed to provide assistance to the action teams with skills and experience not ordinarily available to action teams.

- Approval to action teams, and coordination with functional units, for the action teams to feed forward fixes and enhancements to functional organization units that deliver those MOTS.

- Requests to the steering committee for resolution on stalemates arising between the SQ task force and units of the functional organization.

The role of the policies, practices and procedures task force

The PPP task force interacts with the managers in the functional organization who are responsible for formulating policies, practices and procedures. The purpose is to cause PPPs to become "customer friendly" whenever it will increase customer satisfaction or loyalty.

In addition, in organizations striving to be "customer focused" or "customer driven," the PPP task force will examine internal polices, practices and procedures to ensure that they are also "employee friendly."

Inputs

- Customer feedback from the measurement task force on policies, practices or procedures that negatively affect customer satisfaction or loyalty.

- Requests from action teams to review or revise policies, practices or procedures proposed as part of a fix or an enhancement for a high impact MOT.

- Requests for concurrence with proposed new policies, practices and procedures about to be established by units of the functional organization.

- Requests to the measurement task force to solicit customer reactions to proposed new PPPs.

- Feedback from front-line training sessions that capture policies, practices and procedures that are barriers to good service.

Outputs

- Approval for action teams to use the suggested new and improved PPPs in testing customer satisfaction for MOTs being managed.

- Approval to action teams to feed forward changed PPPs to functional units when a MOT has been fixed or enhanced.

- Requests for steering committee resolution of stalemate situations where the functional organization managers and the shadow organizational managers cannot reach agreement.

The steering committee (or committees)

The steering committee is a cross-functional group of senior managers responsible for implementing the mandate to improve service quality in a manner consistent with the selected goal state.

Any organization with highly autonomous sub-units is a candidate for more than one steering committee. Multiple steering committees make sense where the two autonomous units have little or no interaction or involvement with each other.

For example, in a large bank the trust department and the commercial departments are largely autonomous and have little interaction. However, I wouldn't suggest separate steering committees, because both units are parts of the same functional organization, they share the same resources, and customers could overlap.

Another large bank holding company might be organized into two separate entities. Each entity is completely autonomous, and there is no sharing of resources or overlap of customers. In this case, it would make sense to have two separate steering committees as well as two senior management teams.

The role of the steering committee

The steering committee will create and monitor the shadow organization consistent with the mandate. It will integrate all service quality improvement efforts within the organization. This probably will include existing efforts, as well as those related to the current mandate.

Inputs to the steering committee

- The mandate from senior management will create the steering committee and define the scope, duration and desired timetable of the service quality improvement effort.

- Free access to assessment data (except that which may have been gathered under promise of confidentiality), about the present state of customer satisfaction and loyalty, as well as assessments of how well service quality is being managed at present.

- Reports from each of the task forces designed to keep the steering committee informed on all task force activities.

- Requests for resolution of stalemates between units of the functional organization and the shadow organization.

- Requests for additional resources or budget allocations that may be required to fix or enhance high impact MOTs.

- Customer feedback from the measurement task force. Feedback will combine both raw and summarized feedback.

Outputs from the steering committee

- Creation of the task forces, empowerment of the task forces, and staffing of the task forces.

- Clear communication to the functional organization on the chosen goal state, the mission, the duration and the future of the shadow organization.

- The steering committee will, in conjunction with the senior management team, formulate and communicate a clear vision of the desired goal state and, if appropriate, the desired service strategy for building customer loyalty.

- Prompt approvals or denials for additional resources and or budget allocations when requested by task forces.

- Prompt resolution of stalemates between the shadow and functional organizations.

- Regular reports to the senior management team on progress relating to the mandate.

The senior management team

The senior management team is the only formal unit that is formally part of the functional organization as well as the shadow organization. Thus, the senior management team needs to conduct itself so as to be consistent with the culture, needs, and processes of both sub-organizations.

The role of the senior management team

The role of the team is to assess the existing state of customer satisfaction and loyalty. Based on that assessment, the team will issue a mandate. The mandate will make clear the desired goal state, and any changes to the mission.

Inputs to the senior management team

- The senior management team will sponsor and receive a formal assessment of the current state of service quality.

- The senior management team will examine alternative goal states, changes to the mission, and alternative ways of using shadow organizations to achieve organizational change.
- The senior management team will solicit input from the major stakeholders of the organization about support for organizational change to achieve improved customer loyalty through improved service quality.
- The senior management team will receive regular updates from the steering committee on progress relating to the service quality initiative.

Outputs from the senior management team

The senior management team will:

- issue and define the mandate to the organization.
- define changes, if any are needed, in the mission of the organization.
- define the steering committee, and empower it to form the necessary shadow organization.
- define the desired goal state, which will determine the duration and future of the shadow organization.
- approve or deny requests from the steering committee for resources or budgets necessary to improve service quality.
- communicate and demonstrate its commitment to the chosen goal state and to the service quality initiative.
- model, in its behavior and its decisions, the customer-focused behavior that it seeks to have throughout the entire organization.

The functional organization

The functional organization is the original organization from which the shadow organization was drawn. In most situations, it will continue to operate as it has, except where changes are imposed upon it by the work of the shadow organization.

The role of the functional organization

The role of the functional organization is to conduct business as usual while the shadow organization is interacting with it to gradually improve service quality.

Depending on the desired goal state, people in the functional organization will be preparing for a return to business as usual sometime in the future, or the permanent introduction of a shadow organization, or the eventual transition to a new organizational form.

Inputs to the functional organization

The functional organization will:

- receive clear communications from the communications task force, from the steering committee, and from senior management about the effort to improve service quality.

- receive regular requests for cooperation with the shadow organization as existing work processes are changed to improve customer satisfaction.

- feed forward from moments of truth successfully piloted by action teams.

Outputs from the functional organization

- The functional organization will produce its normal, business as before, delivery of products and services to customers.

- Upon receiving feed forward from task teams who have successfully improved service quality, the functional organization will support the implementation of the new changes throughout all service-providing units.

FIRING ON ALL CYLINDERS
The Service/Quality System for High-Powered Corporate Performance
Jim Clemmer
with Barry Sheehy and Achieve International/Zenger-Miller Associates
Co-published by ASQC Quality Press/Business One Irwin
A practical map for improving service and quality within your organization. You'll find thought-provoking questions that help you analyze what components are amiss within your organization so you and your management team remove quality improvement roadblocks. Jim Clemmer provides essential implementation checklists, "how-to" tips, and deployment processes so you can use Achieve International's Service/Quality System™ to guide your company's continuous quality improvement journey.
ISBN: 1-55623-704-9

SECOND TO NONE
How Our Smartest Companies Put People First
Charles Garfield
Discover how you can create a workplace where both people and profits flourish! *Second to None* by Charles Garfield, the best-selling author of *Peak Performers*, gives you an inside look at today's leading businesses and how they became masters at expanding the teamwork and creativity of their work force. Using this unique mix of practical strategies gleaned from our smartest companies, you can respond to the challenges of today's global marketplace, provide superior service to your customers—and your own employees, maintain a competitive edge during times of rapid transition and restructuring, and much more!
ISBN: 1-55623-360-4

CLOSE TO THE CUSTOMER
25 Management Tips from the Other Side of the Counter
James H. Donnelly, Jr.
Dual Main Selection of the BusinessWeek Book Club!
Based on the actual experiences of the author and others, this sometimes shocking, often humorous look at encounters between customers and organizations gives you 25 ideas you can use to keep your customers coming back for more.
ISBN: 1-55623-569-0

QUALITY IN AMERICA
How to Implement a Competitive Quality Program
V. Daniel Hunt
Dramatically improve your firm's performance, market share, and profitability by implementing a quality improvement program that fits your specific needs. Hunt gives you the unique benefits of leading quality methods, including the Deming Philosophy, the Juran Approach, the Crosby School, the Total Quality Management Concept, and his own "Quality First" methodology so you can overcome quality hurdles in your firm.
ISBN: 1-55623-536-4

SELF-DIRECTED WORK TEAMS
The New American Challenge
Jack B. Orsburn, Linda Moran, Ed Musselwhite, and John H. Zenger
Show employees from diverse areas of your company how to work together more efficiently so your firm can compete more effectively! Includes case histories from TRW, Cummins Engine, General Electric, Blue Cross of Ohio, Hughes Tool, and many others.
ISBN: 1-55623-341-8

Available at fine bookstores and libraries everywhere.